JOHN RICHARDSON worked for mc
coffee-bar and restaurant industry,
largest sandwich business in Ireland.

write *Wake Up and Smell the Profit: 52 Guaranteed Ways to Make More Money in Your Coffee Business* and *The Coffee Boys Step-by-Step Guide to Setting Up and Managing Your Own Coffee Bar*. A keen golfer, he lives with his wife and daughter in Bangor, Northern Ireland.

If you'd like to learn more about the various techniques
and practice drills that I used during the year, go to
www.dreamongolf.com.
I have lots of free videos and further explanation of some
of the slightly more unusual techniques I used.

You can also follow me on Twitter:
www.twitter.com/breakpargolf

PRAISE FOR 'DREAM ON'

'[*Dream On* is] a great heart-warming story, and one which is told with clear-eyed honesty and self-deprecating humour. Read it and see how you can turn your own golfing dreams into reality.'

Irish Independent

'It is very rare that someone achieves a feat like John has done. It is a testimony to him and the way he has applied himself so diligently. These techniques work and I am thrilled to have been of some help to John in his unique and inspiring quest. His results should be an inspiration to golfers at ALL levels. This is dreaming with a PLAN of ACTION.'

Karl Morris, European Tour Mind Coach, www.golf-brain.com

'For golfers [John's] achievement is already being marvelled at and studiously picked over for any nugget of information that will help them improve.'

Irish News

'*Dream On* is fast becoming the most talked-about sports novel of 2009.'

County Down Spectator

'DREAM ON'

One Hacker's Challenge to Break Par in a Year

JOHN RICHARDSON

BLACKSTAFF PRESS BELFAST

First published in 2009 by
Blackstaff Press
4c Heron Wharf, Sydenham Business Park
Belfast, BT3 9LE
with the assistance of
The Arts Council of Northern Ireland

Reprinted 2009 (twice), 2010

Typeset by CJWT Solutions, St Helens

Printed in England by Cromwell Press Group

A CIP catalogue record for this book is available from the British Library

ISBN 978 0 85640 841 0

www.blackstaffpress.com
www.dreamongolf.com

For Seve Ballesteros

Somehow I can't believe there are any heights that can't be scaled by a man who knows the secret of making dreams come true. This special secret, it seems to me, can be summarized in four Cs. They are Curiosity, Confidence, Courage, and Constancy and the greatest of these is Confidence. When you believe a thing, believe it all the way, implicitly and unquestionably.

WALT DISNEY

Contents

Prologue
'Dream On'

Stuart stood quietly and waited for his moment. It had been a long and exhilarating day. He had played a full round of golf at the legendary Royal County Down course, frequently voted one of the top five courses in the world, and situated at the foot of the Mountains of Mourne in Newcastle. It was a Jaguar corporate event and Stuart had been lucky enough to be paired with, and entertained by, local television presenter and golf enthusiast Gerry Kelly. But that hadn't been the main highlight. The big high point of the day had been the chance to play the par-three tenth hole with Ryder Cup star and all-round golfing hero Sam Torrance. Sam had, needless to say, played the hole effortlessly but nerves had got the better of Stuart and, embarrassingly, he managed to top the ball down the fairway. Thankfully, an excellent pitch and a long-holed putt had saved par and he was left with some great but all-too-brief memories of playing with one of Scotland's greatest golfers.

Back in the clubhouse, Stuart's face was burning slightly from the sun and wind. The two pints of Guinness he had just consumed probably enhanced his glow. But he had to stay focused. He was on a mission. He wanted to speak to Sam again but didn't want to appear a pest. The speeches were over and Sam had entertained the audience with some brilliant and hilariously

1

frank opinions on all things golfing. Now he was sitting at the bar having a quiet drink.

Stuart hovered nearby, slightly nervous. The last thing Sam would want to do was answer yet more questions, particularly a somewhat ludicrous and hypothetical question like the one that Stuart was about to ask him. Sam Torrance did not have a reputation for suffering fools gladly, and wondering if he was a fool for doing this, Stuart approached the bar with a sense of trepidation.

'Sam, do you mind if I ask you a quick question?' he blurted out.

Sam smiled and replied, 'Sure, fire away. How can I help you?'

'Well, it's a slightly odd situation really. I have a friend, a guy called John, who is undertaking a golf challenge. He has a full-time job and a wife and child and he's trying to shoot a level-par round or better within a year.'

Sam raised an eyebrow quizzically, prompting Stuart to continue.

'He's really just a hacker now. When he started this challenge he couldn't break 100. So he's trying to take thirty-three strokes off his game in one year and he asked me to find out your opinion on that.'

Sam laughed, then slowly contemplated the question. 'Well, you can tell him from me to dream on.'

'Well, you can't say fairer than that,' Stuart said. 'Can he quote you on that?'

'Oh yes, absolutely.'

'Thank you very much. I'll not take up any more of your time.'

Stuart moved away and smiled as some other golfers started crowding round Sam again, hoping for more tales of how we thrashed the Americans in the Ryder Cup.

It was a perfect answer. If he were honest, it was exactly how Stuart had felt about the challenge to begin with. But he'd known me a long time and had witnessed a few of my 'daft' ideas in action before. Some of them had worked, and some hadn't. He'd seen me start up businesses that had been extremely successful, but he'd also watched, bewildered, as I had created other enterprises that were about as profitable as burning twenty-pound notes.

This was different, though. This was a sporting challenge and, as a keen golfer himself, Stuart wanted to go along for the ride. He'd watched my progress in the first few months and was starting to feel that, despite what Sam had just said, maybe, just maybe, with a following wind and everything else acting in my favour, there might be a chance I would pull it off ...

An Idea and a Dream

Dream no small dreams for they have no power to
move the hearts of men.

JOHANN VON GOETHE

'Tony?'

'Yes, John.'

'How quickly did Mark McMurray get down to scratch?'

'Well, I think he had played a little as a teenager but when
he started again a couple of years ago, his first handicap was 17.
Within eighteen months he had shot a 67 and was playing
off 4.'

'Bloody hell! That is totally unheard of, isn't it? I mean, how
many other people have you seen do that?'

'Absolutely none. Not even close. But don't forget, Mark was
an exceptional basketball player. He could have gone to the
States and played professionally. He had the discipline required
to get better and, probably more importantly, he understood the
psychology of sport. And he had a very obvious natural talent
from day one.'

'Yeah – but it's still a great story, isn't it? It's a great example
of what can be done if you really work at it. Wouldn't it be
interesting to see if you could take somebody else through a
specific process and get that type of improvement? Take a complete beginner and turn them into a scratch player within a year.
From scratch to scratch. Now that *would* be a great story.'

'Not possible. The way the handicap system works, you just couldn't do it in that time-frame.'

'OK. Well, how about this? A beginner or at least a proper hacker, say, a real 24-handicapper, turns into a golfer who can shoot par within a year. Ignore handicaps; he or she just has to shoot one par round within the year. Is that possible?'

'Well, it's certainly an interesting idea. It would have to be somebody with time on their hands. Maybe somebody who doesn't work and had excelled at some other sport beforehand. A trust-fund guy would be good.'

'But that's unrepresentative of most golfers. Ideally, it should be somebody in the same position as an ordinary club golfer – you know, with a job and family.'

'Yeah sure, but that makes it a whole lot harder. They'd need to be really committed. I reckon they'd need to dedicate at least fifteen hours a week to the project.'

'But there must be another Mark out there somewhere ...'

And so it began. A simple conversation at work like so many simple conversations every day in so many offices, bars or coffee shops around the world. You could substitute almost any sport or hobby, but on that particular day it was about golf. Tony White was the golf professional at Blackwood Golf Centre just outside Bangor in County Down, and I had the catering franchise for the bar. We shared an office and this was just another random fantasy that allowed us to avoid doing any work, sparked off by the exceptional golfing prowess of Mark McMurray, our mutual friend. Mark had since gone on to achieve great success as an amateur golfer and held the course record at one local club.

At this stage I had no interest in playing golf myself. I had played a lot as a teenager, but now, in my late twenties, I had very little spare time. I was heavily involved in a variety of food businesses, apart from the golf club bar, including a restaurant and a fish-and-chip shop. I was striving, with a fair number of hiccups, to make my millions but was endlessly fascinated by challenges. I had recently married Lesley, who was in the process of setting up her own PR agency. We had no children as yet and enjoyed a very busy social life. I still had an interest in the game, but it was something I imagined I would take up again some time in the future – when I was older and had those millions safely stashed away.

So, like many conversations of this type, the notion remained an idle fantasy. Then Tony emigrated to Australia and I soon forgot about it.

Or almost. The concept kept drifting around at the back of my mind. About five years later I brought it up again. This time I was having a chat with Debbie Hanna, the Professional Golfers' Association (PGA) pro who had replaced Tony at Blackwood. I asked her what she thought about the idea. She was cautiously positive. She, too, was interested in the notion of the 'challenge', and felt it could be useful PR for the golf centre if it was successful.

'I might just do it myself when I get older and have more time,' I joked.

It was a throwaway remark, but, again, the idea took root at the back of my mind.

Between the ages of nine and sixteen I grew up in the little town of Portstewart on Northern Ireland's north coast, and I will always feel a strong tie to the place. Portstewart has two golf courses and a strong golf culture for children. I'd been bitten by the 'golfing bug' early and even got my handicap down as low as 15 by the time I was fifteen, albeit based on playing the very easy par-64 course.

When I first started, playing golf was simply a way for my mum to get my brother Patrick and me out of the house during the summer holidays and to stop us fighting. These days, we read about Tiger Woods's dedication to practice and how intensely he worked at his game when he was only ten or eleven. For Tiger, messing about at golf involved learning amazing golf tricks, like how to keep the ball up using his sand wedge and hitting it as if it were a baseball.

Messing about at golf for me and my friends when we were young, however, was an altogether more juvenile pursuit. We'd play the first ten holes of the course and then head into one of the adjoining fields to enjoy a game of KooPaa. KooPaa was not, in hindsight, my finest hour. We'd walk through the fields, looking for cowpats of a certain age and consistency. The perfect specimen would have a hard crusty skin but be nice and squishy inside. When you found a good one, the trick was to jump on it, shouting 'KooPaa', without getting your legs covered in dung. The object of the game, rather, was for your chosen cow-pat to splurt its gooey contents all over your friends. The only warning was the 'KooPaa' shout, and if you heard that fateful battlecry you ran for your life. But you didn't always make it. Like I say, not my finest hour, and possibly a fairly good indica-tion of the level of dedication I had to the sport at this stage.

But then, over two glorious summers when I was fifteen and sixteen, I suddenly 'got' golf. One of the original KooPaa gang had moved away to the bright lights of Belfast, and Patrick, who is a year older than me, started to lose interest in the game. For the first time I'd found a sport that I was better at than him, and he didn't enjoy being beaten by me. In his defence, I probably enjoyed the thrill of beating him a bit too much, and in the end he drifted away from golf. But thankfully two of my best school buddies, Robert Murphy and Roy Nichol, got into golf just at that time and the three of us started to work pretty hard at the game.

Robert, Roy and I would meet every day on the 'wee course' and play one, sometimes two, rounds. We'd sit in the little club-house afterwards with a can of Lilt and a packet of Peanut Treats and talk about our golfing heroes. This was the glory time of Seve Ballesteros who had already won his first British Open and who was taking the golfing world by storm. Like Arnold Palmer before him, and Tiger Woods today, Seve was changing the face of golf and creating a whole new wave of interest in the sport. We would sit around and dream about getting to one of the tournaments to see this demi-god play and ponder what it would take to make it as a professional golfer.

I started to buy *Golf World* every month with my pocket money and I'd drive my family nuts with fantastical commen-taries on my fabulous win in the British Open: 'We meet John at home relaxing with his parents after his recent success. This young man came from nowhere to beat the greatest in the world and win the Open at St Andrews. Even the great Spaniard himself, Severiano Ballesteros, was humbled by John's amazing control ...' I'd spend time out on the course on my own, pretending I was Seve and commentating on the round in his Spanish accent. I'd comment on each shot as if a TV camera was alongside me, covering the match just like the celebrity Pro-Ams they used to have on television: 'I heet a very good drive down the fairway, just a leetle to the righ'. Now I need to heet it to the righ'-han' side of the green and let it float down. I very confident in thees type of sho'.'

I remember telling my parents, and anyone else who would listen, that I wanted to become a professional golfer when I left school. The simple fact was, however, that I wasn't good enough. I never got any better than a 15 handicap and there were loads of kids my age who were playing off single-figure handicaps. Today's mentality of encouraging your kids that they can be anything they want to be didn't really exist then. My father had wanted to be a pilot since he was a small boy, for instance, but couldn't fulfil his dream because his eyesight wasn't good enough. It was a classic example of how you can't always be anything you want to be, because sometimes there will be a physical barrier to it. He had gone on to have a successful career in the furniture trade but there's no doubt that his heart was always in flying and in later years he bought a glider and still uses it every weekend. My parents certainly didn't laugh at my dream, but it was made pretty clear that achieving it was highly unlikely.

Of course, it didn't help that I had a natural disposition to always look for the easy way out. Most teenagers have seminal moments where they suddenly realise the value of hard graft and finally start to grow up. This didn't happen to me until much later in life. Instead, my seminal moment came from the opposite perspective, while watching an old Terry Thomas movie from the early 1960s. *School for Scoundrels*, based on the Stephen Potter *One Upmanship* and *Lifemanship* books, is the story of how a naive guy is schooled in all sorts of ways to win back the girl who dumped him, without doing any real hard graft himself. To me that seemed like bliss. Drifting through life as a bit of a chancer without ever having to succumb to the tedium of work. Amazing! And if I could apply that principle to my golf, well, what a solution! A sort of Terry Thomas plays the PGA tour scenario. I spent more time imagining how this might happen than getting out on the course and properly practising my game. No big surprise then that I didn't really improve.

One day Robert arrived at the course and wowed us all with a brilliant idea. It was the summer of 1983. In a few weeks Ballesteros was coming to Dublin to play in the Irish Open. About 150 miles south of Portstewart, Dublin could be reached by two relatively simple train journeys, and Robert said that we could stay the night in a wee bed-and-breakfast. Why didn't we go and see him?

I could hardly wait to get home and suggest it to my parents. Since we were fifteen, there was an element of concern, but with a bit of persuading, they agreed. So, on a bright and sunny summer morning, the three amigos travelled to Belfast to board the Enterprise, bound for Dublin's Connolly Station and Seve. We spent the journey high on the freedom of our first real holiday adventure without our parents and passed the time discussing the undisputed delights of Victoria Principal or singing a song Robert had picked up somewhere. When I think about that day, the words of Bagatelle's 'Summer in Dublin' still run round my head:

> So I jumped on a bus to Dún Laoghaire,
> Stopping off to pick up my guitar,
> And a drunk on the bus told me how to get rich,
> I was glad we weren't going too far.

The sight of Seve in the flesh was incredible. He was playing with Bernhard Langer, his great European rival in those days. We were all utterly starstruck, in absolute awe of the gobsmacking presence that the charismatic Seve projected when he walked onto the tee. I remember looking at the size of his forearms and then glancing down at my own weedy teenage ones and realising that I had a *lot* of growing up to do. And Seve didn't disappoint, conquering yet another title right there in front of our eyes. Even now, twenty-five years later, I have never been in the presence of such a powerful personality. He literally oozed control, power and magnetism.

It had been a magical trip, but we messed up the theoretically simple return journey. We arrived at Belfast's Central Station with one easy train change to make for the last sixty miles back home. An easy thing to do. Take the train to Portstewart. But never underestimate the stupidity of teenage boys with minds full of a potent mix of Seve Ballesteros, on the one hand, and Victoria Principal, on the other. We got on the wrong train and ended up heading somewhere else we shouldn't have been going.

Once we realised our mistake, we got off at the first available stop, and after a few frantic phone calls we ended up staying with Robert's auntie in Lisburn. But none of this mattered, at least not to us, anyway. We had seen Seve in the flesh. We had left Portstewart as boys but we were returning feeling more like men … or so we thought. Maybe, just maybe, some of that Seve magic would rub off on our own games.

I continued to dream my dream of becoming a professional golfer, but everyone I mentioned it to responded with the same line: 'To be a professional, you'd need to be playing off scratch already.' Of course they were correct, but deep down I knew that I did have some basic ability, and if I'd had any 'stick-at-it-ness', as my mother calls it, I'd have done something to try to prove them wrong.

But the teenage years are an odd time. Gradually, you become more interested in fitting in. Not appearing foolish. Wanting to be accepted. It's a rare teenager that has the ability or drive to keep pursuing a goal that everyone around them says is foolish. Sadly, I wasn't made of that mettle.

But then, nobody ever sat me down and said: 'John – becoming a golf professional is very difficult, but it certainly isn't impossible. You have a long, long way to go, though. What you need to do is rush home from school every day and do your homework as fast and as well as you can, then spend the rest of the night practising. Forget about watching television and playing with your mates. You'll need to practise, practise, practise, and then practise some more. Why don't you try that for three months and see how you get on? Then make the big decision.'

If they had, well I might just have rejected the easy option and taken their advice.

Procrastination

> Man, alone, has the power to transform his thoughts into physical reality; man, alone, can dream and make his dreams come true.
>
> NAPOLEON HILL

So instead of taking action, I just let the dream drift. I stopped talking about it for fear of making a fool of myself and continued to play golf just for fun. And then, when I was sixteen, we moved to Belfast. The dream of a golfing career very quickly turned into the more immediate pleasures of beer and girls.

My new friends didn't play golf and the club I joined was all about wearing jackets and ties and making business contacts. But among the membership was a certain girl who was better than I could ever dream of being. Debbie Hanna – someone who many years later would play a vital role in my challenge – was winning tournaments left, right and centre, and had more golfing talent in her little finger than I had in my entire body. A girl! And she wasn't even as old as me. It was obvious she had raw talent, so what was the point of me making any effort when I would never be as good as that? Of course, I didn't bother to clock that she often spent nine straight hours practising on the range.

All this proved a convenient excuse to put my dream on hold and put golf in general firmly on the back boiler. So the years drifted by, and I went for very long periods of time without hitting a ball at all. I went to university in England to study for a degree in business and marketing but, more importantly, to continue to explore the delights of girls and beer, and to sit up to five in the morning with my student friends putting the world to rights. On my return to Belfast in the early 1990s, I set up a sandwich business with a close friend. We were maverick entrepreneurs, who were initially incredibly successful, but, ultimately, in an act of stunning naiveté, we lost our proverbial shirts. I certainly had no time for golf or stuffy old golf clubs.

My ability to shoot a round in the 90s soon drifted into an inability to break 100. I lost all contact with Robert and Roy and the golf scene in general, and became a typical hacker. Even when I was sharing an office with Tony I wasn't inspired to play better golf – or to play more often. Each time I had to attend a business or social function where golf was played, I'd bash my way around, losing balls, feeling embarrassed and frustrated. I'd be elated at the odd straight drive or crisply struck iron but these were always mixed in with 90-odd shots of mediocrity and tedious thrashing around in the rough. I'd played enough as a child to know that golf is a vastly more enjoyable game when you are playing well. Even then, it can be maddening, but it's much less frustrating than shooting 9s or 10s, swearing like Gordon Ramsay and holding everybody else up.

By the summer of 2000, the millions had yet to arrive, but I had picked myself up from the collapse of the sandwich business and was running a couple of chip shops, had a small stake in a restaurant and held the catering franchise for the golf club. Lesley and I had been married for four years and we now had a beautiful baby daughter, Aimee, who seemed to have an incredibly poor grasp of the need for sleep. I was very busy and playing golf more sporadically than ever. During that summer, not one of my rounds broke 100. I was so mortified that, on a couple of occasions, I worked very hard to try to string together a decent round, only to card a score closer to 110. It was deeply humiliating and hugely frustrating.

During 2001 and 2002, I began to think once more about the challenge Tony and I had discussed all those years ago – of scoring a level-par round within a year – and about the possibility of doing it myself. With a very busy working life, still no millions in the bank and Lesley and Aimee to think of, the circumstances were far from ideal. Nevertheless, I gradually started to formulate a coherent plan. Due to the miserable winter weather we have in Northern Ireland, I believed that the time to start such a challenge would be September. That would provide six wintry months to concentrate on developing a swing and grooving it in on the range. It would also allow me time to read up on all the theory and investigate the mental side of the game, which I was convinced held much of the key to success.

Playing on course on any kind of regular basis would be pretty much out of the question, since most courses move to temporary tees and greens during these months. I knew from running the bar that the course at Blackwood was even likely to be closed for days at a stretch if it rained too hard.

After six months of theory and range practice, I'd be left with six full months to put all this into action on the course. It sounded great in principle; logically it should work. Keeping away from the course in the early part of the challenge would actually be a bonus, as it would avoid the distraction and intimidation of play until I had a repeatable swing and decent ball-striking ability.

I discussed the project with the management at the golf centre and they were generous in their support. I was friendly with Richard Gibson, general manager of the centre, and he could see that there would be great media coverage if we succeeded. I could play the course free of charge and they would allow me free use of the range. It all seemed to be falling into place. Debbie Hanna even volunteered to coach me.

Except ... I did what most people do – I circled. I acted like a scared hyena waiting to get the remains of the lions' kill. September came and went and came and went again and I still didn't get started. The time wasn't right ... Things at work were a bit hectic ... I wasn't fit enough ... Excuse after excuse piled up and of course when I'd missed my September deadline there was no point in starting until the following year.

Half-heartedly I planned to start in September of 2003 and

again just cruised past the deadline, but this time I was mentally much closer to the project than I had been before. I bought a few golf magazines and marvelled at how much the technology had moved on. Huge titanium driver heads, easy-to-hit cavity back irons, and wonder balls capable of going huge distances. Lob wedges, gap wedges and hybrid clubs. It seemed that the market had gone mad. But I found it all fascinating and could feel my interest in golf rekindling.

I'm an avid reader and have always believed in the power of books when there has been any problem or challenge in my life. Generally somebody somewhere will have been through a similar problem and invariably will have written a book about it. I suffer from arthritis in my hip joints and in the mid-nineties it had become really bad. I had reached a stage where I was in permanent pain and had started to develop a noticeable limp. My father had recently had his hip joint replaced and since I was ten years younger than he was before he had any arthritic pain at all, I felt the future looked bleak. I certainly didn't want to be looking at replacement surgery before I was forty and that seemed to be the basis of conventional treatments. So out came the alternative medicine books. I read many books on natural cures for arthritis and although I didn't follow any one of them to the letter, I took on board the common strands and created a diet for myself that I've pretty much stuck to ever since. The pain, although not a thing of the past by any means, has become controllable and when my hips do get sore it is usually my own fault, brought on by failing to follow my diet, putting on weight, not getting enough sleep, or drinking too much wine.

So as I thought more about the challenge, I surfed Amazon, searching for books that I thought might help. Initially I settled on a couple of books by Bob Rotella, the pre-eminent sports psychologist and performance consultant. At this stage, I was more interested in what was possible than in the specifics of swings, and his books fitted the bill. I soon discovered a mind-boggling statistic that became a recurring theme in many of the books I subsequently read.

Forty years ago the average handicap was 17. Today the

average handicap is ... 17. So, the vast developments in golf-club and ball technology has made not one jot of difference to the average golfer. And all the increased understanding of sporting psychology hasn't made a difference either. Nor has wall-to-wall, twenty-four-hour television coverage on the Golf Channel. Professionals like Tiger Woods, Vijay Singh and Phil Mickelson may have brought the old courses of the world to their knees with new technology and their understanding of fitness and sport psychology but average golfers appear to be getting more and more frustrated. They are playing as badly as ever but losing vastly more expensive balls and getting caught up in the preposterous merry-go-round of buying £300 drivers every other year.

I found Rotella's books inspirational and quickly read everything else he had published on the subject. *The Golf of Your Dreams*, which is about how to become a better golfer, was particularly helpful. It even has a short section about getting to a scratch handicap. According to Rotella, it isn't possible to get to scratch in less than two years and only then with a huge amount of work. Here was a chink of light. I wasn't trying to get to scratch. I simply wanted to score one level-par round. A very different thing. I was more than happy to put the work in and was now in a better position to do it.

Rotella is a very private man who is difficult to get hold of. I managed, however, to e-mail Robert Cullen, a writer who has co-authored a number of books with Rotella. I asked him for his views on the likely success of my challenge. He wished me well but felt that it would be a minimum of eighteen months before I could achieve the round. Again, that was another chink of light for me – in my naivety I couldn't see much difference between twelve months and eighteen months. I'd just work harder and smarter than he expected.

The momentum continued to build. Timothy Gallwey's *Inner Game of Golf* was influential. As a tennis coach, his seminal work, *The Inner Game of Tennis*, had wide-reaching implications for many sports. A friend of mine had even been advised to read it as an aid to his piano practice. A mediocre but keen golfer, Gallwey believed that by applying these techniques to his game he could break 80 within a year. That really struck a chord. The premise wasn't exactly the same as mine, but it was close enough to reinforce my belief that success was possible.

Along with all this reading around the subject of golf, I read an inspirational book entitled *It's a Long Way from Penny Apples* by Bill Cullen, the Irish entrepreneur and philanthropist. Cullen and his brothers and sisters (fourteen in all) grew up in crushing poverty in the Dublin slums. Through incredibly hard work, he succeeded in changing his grim situation and is now one of the wealthiest men in Ireland. This is no ego-driven, you-can-make-a-fortune self-help book. It is a beautifully written story of overcoming the odds and making something of your life. The enormity of his achievement made my little quest to play a level-par round look ludicrously simple by comparison.

These days the Internet and the motivational market are filled with people telling you how to be rich or slim or more successful. Many such gurus have actually achieved nothing in their own lives. In books and seminars they peddle a dream, and convince many individuals that their lives will change for ever if only they would follow a few magic steps. The power of such hype may last for a week or two, then reality bites once more. Then the next guru comes along with another I'll-sort-your-life-out solution. And again it's a simple regurgitation of old motivational theory, a slick suit and some excellent marketing. Bill Cullen, by comparison, was an honest-to-goodness *doer*, a breath of fresh air in an over-hyped world. His story inspired me to get out there and work towards the challenge.

I continued reading the golfing bibles, flicking through golf magazines and watching golfing videos. Then, suddenly, something inside me clicked. It became impossible for me *not* to make a start. I'd tipped myself over a precipice and didn't want to talk or read about it any more – I had to *do* it.

This is the way I always work and I believe it's the same for many of us. You have to keep bombarding yourself with sound information and useful ideas about a project until, all of a sudden, you reach a stage where you have to act. You build a tide of momentum and you must jump on that wave and ride it. All at once, the pain of not starting is greater than the pleasure of putting it off.

I knew that come September of that year – 2004 – I would definitely be able to get going. But in mid-May I became frustrated. I had built up too much momentum too soon. I couldn't wait until September. The challenge was dominating my thoughts, the sun was starting to shine and I needed to go. The timing, though, was about as wrong as it could possibly be. Starting in May would mean that I'd be learning during the summer months and playing through the winter. But I knew I had to get going. All that mattered was to start.

I sat down with Lesley and explained that I'd made up my mind to give it a go. I promised that the time spent would be just general evening TV-watching time, and I'd do everything in my power to ensure that it would impact on her and Aimee as little as possible. She was very supportive but I could tell that she was nervous about just how much time it would *actually* take. She had witnessed me becoming obsessive about various business ventures before and could see the parallels.

Not only was the timing wrong in terms of the time of year, it also wasn't ideal for my working life. When I joked with Debbie that I might do the challenge myself, I had a vision of a future utopia where I would only be working thirty hours or so a week. This bore no relation to the reality of my current situation. I'd long since stopped working at Blackwood and had moved on to become a director and shareholder of Northern Ireland's fastest-growing garden-centre group. We had two sites, plans for three more, and a total staff of 120. I was travelling thirty thousand miles a year between the sites and working at least a fifty-hour week.

Add to that scenario a busy family life and an active social life, and it was evident there was little spare time for self-indulgent projects like this. According to the criteria I laid down at the outset, the challenge would only be deemed a success if I completed the level-par round, remained married and kept my job. Naively, I just expected that it would all work out.

I phoned a bemused Debbie and talked it through.

'I've really got to start,' I blurted out.

She paused. 'OK ... You mean this September?'

'No, I mean now. I've reached a peak of excitement and I have to get going.'

Another pause.

'But John, your timing is about as wrong as it can get! You're going to make life extremely difficult for yourself.'

'I know, I know all that.' I was concerned that she thought it was utter madness on my part. 'I just can't wait, though. I think the moment is right psychologically and I really need to get out there. I've been putting it off for far too long and at this rate I'm going to end up on my deathbed still promising I'll do it next year.'

Silence.

'So, can you come out and play soon and we'll treat that as the first round? Help me put together a control round that we can use as the starting point?'

She laughed. 'OK, OK, I think you're mad but let me check my diary.'

I felt as eager as an eight-year-old before a school trip to the zoo.

'How about next Wednesday?' she said.

'Perfect. I really appreciate it, Debbie. See you then.'

I was beside myself with excitement.

We're Off!

The way to get started is to quit talking and
begin doing.

WALT DISNEY

So, on Wednesday 26 May 2004, I made a start. There are two
eighteen-hole courses at Blackwood – a simple par three, and a
proper par seventy-one called the Hamilton. Standing on the first
tee of the Hamilton that morning, I was horribly nervous. I told
myself that, theoretically, this round didn't matter. It was just the
control round to gauge my level, but of course it wasn't quite as
simple as that. I still had to satisfy Debbie that I had the potential
to win the challenge. She would be looking for something in my
game that would convince her that it was worth coming along for
the ride. After all, she would be giving her time free of charge. If
I played a round that was too bad, she could easily decide that it
just wasn't going to be possible, no matter how strongly I
believed in the successful outcome of the project.

Debbie is a naturally positive, motivated and driven person
who values achievement. She had played on the European
Ladies' Professional Golf Association (LPGA) tour for six years
and saw at first hand just what can be accomplished with hard
work, practice and discipline. As a teacher, she admires anyone
who wants to improve their game. Unfortunately, however, she
also sees hundreds of golfers every year with lofty improvement
goals, very few of whom actually see them through. When the

realisation hits home that hard work and lots of practice are essential, most players tend to give up and go back to their old ways. I had to prove to her that not only was I capable of sticking at it, but that I wasn't totally devoid of talent and could provide her with a good level from which to work.

An eight on the first hole hardly helped my case. It had been at least a year since I had played and I didn't seem to be able to get it together at all. Nerves were obviously a factor but perhaps more important was the disconcerting notion that I had to *perform*. It suddenly struck me that I now had to play well for somebody other than myself. This is a problem that affects all players to varying degrees out on the course and it was to plague me throughout the year ahead.

A seven on the par-five second hole followed and that certainly didn't help my cause either.

We stood on the third tee and Debbie decided it was time for a chat.

'John, will you just relax please? A bad round at this stage doesn't matter.'

'Er, well, yes. I know. I'm just anxious to show you there is something here that you can work with.'

'There is. I've already seen that, so please relax.' And then she added with a grin. 'This is probably the only time in the year when your score won't matter, so I'd advise you to relax and enjoy it. You won't have this luxury again for a long time.'

It was a valid point and I slowly relaxed and gradually got it together. I took a four at the tough par-three third and then parred the easy par-four fourth. A seven at the next after four putts put any cockiness out of my head, but I came to the turn in 50. To be honest, after I'd calmed down, I was very pleased with how I'd played those nine holes. I was hitting the ball better than I had in a long time and most of my bad shots were the result of nerves.

The back nine was a similar, if slightly worse, story. It's a tougher nine holes than the front and mistakes are more fiercely punished. A whopping ten on the easy eleventh hole with two lost balls and a couple more lost balls on the thirteenth and fourteenth meant I came back in 53. Total score 103. Pretty woeful, but actually quite a good round of golf for me at that stage. I hadn't played a full round where every shot counts and there are no mulligans and gimmes for maybe twenty years, and I'd forgotten just how tough it was to string together a decent stroke score.

So, in one way I was pleased with how I'd played. I felt that I'd demonstrated the basis of a decent swing, and yet it did concern me that what I considered a good round had produced a score of 103. I'd played many rounds worse than that in the previous few years, and truth be told, if I hadn't marked a card, I would have estimated that it was a mid-90s round.

Debbie had not offered any advice, deliberately so, other than to try to calm me down during the round. She wanted to see my game in its raw state. When we sat in the bar afterwards with a cup of coffee, I rather smugly expected her to say that she thought I had a good basic swing. Needless to say, she did nothing of the sort.

She quietly sat and made a list on a piece of notepaper. It went like this:

1 Grip too 'strong' with right hand

2 Ball position too inconsistent

3 Course management

4 Ignoring the elements (wind, etc.)

5 Short game method and technique

6 Putting technique

7 Distance control

8 Visualisation

And at the bottom of the page – Friday, 28 May, 12 p.m. – the date of our first lesson.

We talked about the process and whether she felt I could do it. This was a time for honesty. Debbie had not witnessed anyone accomplish the sort of improvement in the time-frame I was talking about, but she reiterated that she believed it to be possible.

Looking me straight in the eye, she said: 'I know I could do it if I was presented with the challenge, so I do think it's possible.

You're going to have to work extremely hard, though, and it is not going to be easy.'

She held my gaze, closely reading my face, as I attempted to convince her that I would indeed work hard. I could sense there was still some level of doubt in her mind.

However, she knew me well enough to believe that I was capable of seeing a project through from beginning to end. She was aware of my entrepreneurial streak and felt that I had proved in other arenas that I wasn't afraid of a challenge, a quality that boded well for this present one. By the end of our meeting I felt I'd done enough to convince her that I was worth the effort and that I wasn't too caught up in the excitement of it all to be blind to the enormity of the challenge ahead. We were both one hundred per cent committed.

There is a stage of euphoria at the start of any long-promised challenge or goal like this one. You are filled to the brim with a 'can do' attitude. It's all pure possibility. It's a wonderful high, but it doesn't last long. Just watch the heartfelt testimonials that people give after a motivational seminar. They are full of enthusiasm in the belief that their life can be so much better, but they have yet to do any of the hard work that will actually make the change.

And that's where I was. I'd started, the card was in my hand and I'd played quite well. Perhaps more importantly, I'd completed the first big hurdle, which was to convince Debbie that I could do it and that it was a challenge worth taking. The thought of the year ahead was exhilarating. There is a certain romance about imagining the hard graft – before you actually do it. In my mind little movie-style montages of the effort I'd have to go through were playing – me at the gym, straining to lift weights; a lonely session practising my drive on a snow-covered range; pushing myself to the limit jogging along a country road. The fist-pumping as I finally hole the putt on the eighteenth. Flickering images of Rocky preparing for the big fight; runners training for the 100 metres in *Chariots of Fire*. That kind of thing. Ah, the joy of an overly fertile imagination.

I was all go. I was off and running and it was exciting. Delusional, but exciting.

A Taste of Reality

> Twenty years from now you will be more disappointed by the things that you didn't do than by the ones you did do. So throw off the bowlines. Sail away from the safe harbor. Catch the trade winds in your sails. Explore. Dream. Discover.
>
> MARK TWAIN

And so to the first lesson. Filled with this euphoric enthusiasm, I stood at the range with Debbie and hit a few balls. We talked about the teaching process and the frustrations of being a teaching professional giving lessons to dozens of, frankly, lazy golfers every week. People who are after a quick fix. Players who may have developed a slice or a hook and expect the pro to correct their problem in one or two lessons, paying perhaps less than a tenth of what they shelled out for their new driver.

The pro might change the players' swing path or alter their weight distribution, and after a few tough shots, they will start to see a difference. They hit a few more and it all seems to be working. Thank you, thank you, they say. That's brilliant. Much appreciated. You're a great teacher. I've paid for my half-hour and you've fixed my problem. Most of the time the pro will ignore the other fundamental problems of the swing, because it's not what their clients want to address. They aren't prepared to make deep-seated changes to an essentially flawed swing, even though those changes could perhaps turn them into a single-figure handicapper. They have merely applied a band-aid to their temporary problem and it has worked.

The band-aid can help to fix the issue and may create a lasting change but only if the player is prepared to stick at it. The pro will explain the work that needs to be done before they go back out on the course again. It will be essential to practise and hit several buckets of balls, focusing on the advice the professional gave. Generally, though, this doesn't happen. Some may buy another twenty balls and practise the swing for ten, and then muck about trying to hit the fence with the rest. Most simply finish off the dozen or so balls after their lesson and merrily leave the range. Perhaps they have a meeting to go to, or need to get home for their dinner, or maybe they just want to have a pint with their mates. So off they toddle, the excellent advice still fresh in their minds, with a strong intention to visit the range again before they next play.

What they don't do is spend ten minutes writing down the pro's precise instructions so they don't forget, or book another lesson in a week's time to check that all the intended practice is going in the right direction. Frequently, of course, any intention to get back to the range is caught up in 'life' and just doesn't happen. And then Saturday comes around. They've forgotten most of the changes they were taught and certainly haven't grooved them to any level of confidence in their swing. The result? A bad round. Neither fish nor fowl, they use a combination of their old swing and the vague recollection of what their pro taught them. But whose fault is it? Well, certainly not their own. 'It's that bloody pro,' they grumble. 'My swing is ruined.'

I know this story so well because in the past I, too, have blamed professionals for my bad game. My parents had bought me a course of lessons with a professional about ten years previously, after my game had first really started to deteriorate. But he messed up what I believed was my 'natural rhythm' so badly that I didn't even finish the course. Golfers love to talk about this natural rhythm – 'Look at that wee fella on the range. He's pure poetry.' 'Yes – that swing didn't come from a book.' It's easy to ignore the fact that the 'wee fella' has probably hit thousands and thousands of balls and is already working with a coach. Golfers love to believe that some people just have it. Seve didn't help matters. He played in such a swashbuckling way that he convinced many amateurs that his game was borne out of good genes and raw talent. They liked to forget that he spent a childhood creating amazing shots with a hand-me-down three iron on his home course.

But this time it needed to be different for me. I did, rather naively, feel that I had a semblance of a decent golf swing, which, with a few of these band-aids, could be a great swing. In reality, of course, I had nothing that could be turned into a low, single-figure handicapper's swing. We needed to go right back to the beginning, which, if I'm honest, I found almost humiliating. I stood there with Debbie teaching me grip, stance and ball position exactly as Alan Hunter, the local golf professional, had done in Portstewart twenty-five years ago. Surely I was better than that? Er, nope.

The simple fact was that my grip was dreadful. It was much too strong, with my right hand twisted too far round to the right. My clubface was always several degrees open and I seemed to have an entirely random idea as to where to place the ball and position my feet. We stood for the guts of an hour going over this very basic stuff. Not what I'd expected at all. I thought I would get some standard swing tweaks and a lot of practice tips to concentrate on. The concept of having to learn ball position again and how to grip the club was not in my plan, and certainly took some of the wind out of my sails.

Relentlessly addressed in every major golf instructional manual, the importance of the grip cannot be overestimated. These days I stroll along the range and watch bad grip after bad grip and I know, from bitter experience, exactly the sort of effort these golfers will have to put in to get it right. The problem is, the grip is vital, and if it's wrong, it's also one of the hardest things to change and keep changed. My basic grip had been developed more than twenty years previously, and although I hadn't played much in the interim, it was still a grip grooved over two decades.

My other major issue at this stage was that tendency to have my clubface open, with the result that my aim was to the right of the target. Superficially a much easier thing to correct, but, even to this day I still find myself having to check this on a regular basis. It was brought home to me time and again during the challenge year that good golf is at least as much about the way you stand at the ball and prepare to swing as it is about the swing itself. Of course, this may seem a very boring concept and won't sell many magazines or hyped-up Internet instructional manuals. 'Blast your drives 300 yards with the new Fandango 300XTR' will always catch more attention as a headline than 'Check your stance is right and play more accurate golf'.

Telling the World

> You may say I'm a dreamer/ but I'm not the only
> one/ I hope someday you'll join us/ and the world
> will live as one.
>
> JOHN LENNON

Four days after starting the challenge I decided to take the idea to a wider audience. I began posting on a variety of Internet bulletin boards throughout the world to see what people thought about the possibility of my success:

> From Scratch to Scratch in One Year – Possible?
>
> Is it possible, in your opinion, to take a golfer who cannot break 100 to a scratch round of 71 within one year? The golfer in question has a full-time job and a busy family life, restricting practice to a couple of hours a day. He is thirty-seven years of age and of average to poor fitness. The challenge started this week ...
>
> Many thanks,
> John

Several bulletin boards were too quiet to elicit a response, but the main forum that came up on a Google search was Australian, and the uniquely blunt nature of the Australian character quickly came to inspire and motivate me in some very peculiar ways.

Some of the responses were sceptical, others were supportive. 'Is it possible? In my opinion, no.'

'To be honest, I would have to say no ... I say good luck to him, and I hope he proves me wrong, as it would give hope to everyone.'

'I don't know whether he can get to scratch, but the one thing I do know – he won't have a family by forty. (He will have a large monthly alimony, though.)'

'It took someone like Greg Norman almost three years to get ... to scratch, and he was a youngster then, and practised almost the full day.'

'If he has the dedication, and the patience, I can probably see him down to 18, perhaps 14 in a year ... especially with only two hours' practice a day.'

The reality was that the idea of a challenge like this wasn't new to most people in the forum – a few magazines had followed golfers who'd embarked on similar projects without much success. Some forum members had tried to make big improvements themselves. So the general consensus was that it wasn't possible – I was too old and therefore couldn't or wouldn't be prepared fully to put my trust in a golf pro. I was too busy with my job and couldn't commit to my ten or fifteen hours of practice per week. Members of the forum gave long lists of people who had tried and failed to make dramatic improvements.

Entering Internet bulletin boards calls for caution. While there are many genuine contributors, these forums also enable anonymous keyboard warriors – people who wouldn't say boo to a goose in real life – to sit at home and spout aggressively about any subject under the sun. They can also be very cliquey. You may be initially welcomed into the group but very quickly can find yourself isolated if your way of thinking differs radically from dominant views prevalent in the forum.

In my case, polite encouragement and guarded scepticism rapidly turned to stronger cynicism from a couple of members and one in particular shocked me with a vitriolic attack on my challenge. The experience reminded me of Jerry Lewis's brilliant observation: 'When you climb up a flag pole, people are going to see your ass. And they'll want to knock you down, not because THEY want to be up there themselves – but because they don't want YOU to be there.' It seemed that I had yet to strike a ball and here I was upsetting people. But I have a particularly ingrained I'll-bloody-show-you mentality and such aggressive comments merely spurred me on.

In the end, nobody came up with a valid enough reason for the challenge not to work, and there had been enough encouragement to make it seem worthwhile. With my eyes opened to the fact that the whole world wasn't going to be one hundred per cent behind me, I started the hard graft. And hard graft it surely was. Boring graft, too, with a total concentration on the basics for several lessons.

Apart from the grip and the difficulty of that change, my leg movement needed a lot of work. At the range one day Debbie looked at me in amusement.

'What's with the Elvis legs?' she said. 'You need to sort that out if we're to get any consistency here.'

She was right. I had a tendency to swing my legs around, Elvis-fashion. While this may have been a great career move for the King in 1956, certainly guaranteeing him a lot of interest from the ladies, it wasn't quite so effective in the middle of a golf swing.

'Try to rotate more around your spine with a lot less movement,' Debbie added.

She paused, struggling to find a simple analogy that I might grasp.

'A bit less Elvis and a bit more Dalek from *Dr Who*.'

Not perhaps the most scientific of comparisons, but it did give me a clear picture of what I needed to work on. She told me to practise with a football in my hands and turn it round as if I were handing it to somebody beside me. Next time I was out on the range, I kept the image of a Dalek turning running through my mind. And it worked, but I had to bite my tongue to stop myself from shouting, 'Exterminate! Exterminate!'

My ball position, swing plane, and shoulder and hip turn could all be corrected and worked on relatively easily. It's extremely easy to get into overload with the golf swing, however. There are so many factors you need to get right before you even contemplate hitting the ball, that very soon you wonder how you're going to get anywhere at all. To a beginner the swing rapidly becomes a huge mass of movements of seemingly every major body part. To try to get all this together into a fluid movement appears an impossible task. The simplification of these movements is where a good teacher comes in.

One of Debbie's great assets is that she keeps it simple and makes you concentrate on one or two basic things at a time, which avoids confusion. You cannot play well if you are trying to correct two or three things during the swing. It just ain't gonna happen.

So I concentrated on set-up, and swinging with a bit less movement. My main problem lay in my tendency to lock my right knee during the backswing. A very common problem for many golfers, it robs the swing of much of its power.

At this stage I began to look around for quick solutions and easier ways to achieve my goal, and found myself drawn to the Internet again. There was endless reading and advice available. Night after night I sat at the computer, looking for the elusive secret that would improve my golf. Often Lesley would go to bed, and I'd tell her I'd only be five more minutes, truly believing this to be the case. Hours later I'd suddenly realise it was 1.30 a.m. and creep guiltily up the stairs, trying not to wake her. And rarely had I read anything of any real use.

During one of these late-night sessions, however, I found an interesting video for sale. A guy in America, Jim McLellan, claimed that ninety-nine per cent of teaching pros are wrong when it comes to the golf swing. According to him, it needs to be taught in a different way. Despite my usual sceptical reaction to controversial claims on the Internet, there was something that intrigued me about his approach. I bought his video and entered into a bit of dialogue with him. For unlike most of the peddlers of play-better-golf-instantly systems to be found on the Net, Jim was prepared to answer e-mails about his method. Additionally his swing is a masterpiece, so beautifully smooth that it makes Ernie Els's look like that of a 24-handicap hacker. Of course, you have to ask yourself, well, if he's so good why wasn't Jim ever on tour? But I suppose I gave him a by-ball, since people have different priorities.

The swing, for Jim, should be a simple swishing movement. He advises the golfer to disregard much of the very detailed specifics that so many other teachers emphasise. Keep your head still, says Jim, get your hands high on the backswing and high again on the follow-through, and Bob is pretty much your golfing uncle.

The gist of his method is this. Watch the video many times and practise swinging a club without hitting a ball; in fact, ninety per cent of your practice should not involve hitting a ball. This should ideally take place in your garden or backyard and with a weighted club. You should not hit a ball for at least fourteen days and must swing the club for at least five minutes several times a day. You must concentrate on Jim's technique alone – put all other sources of instruction and advice on hold for the duration. And ask someone to video your efforts, he says, so that they can be compared to his swing.

His method sounded fascinating and, although it had hints of too good to be true, I felt that there was some merit in trying it out. Obviously I couldn't, or wouldn't, commit to giving up all other sources of instruction, and, at this stage, I just couldn't keep away from a ball. I did, however, watch his video religiously and swung the club a lot in my back garden. My living room, too. I didn't always succeed in avoiding the light fittings, no matter how hard I tried.

Another factor made me trust Jim's principles. I was standing at the range one evening and playing badly. Much of my initial euphoria had worn off and I didn't seem to be able to hit the ball properly at all. I was caught up in the slog of relentless practice and some days seemed to end up far worse than I was when I started.

Hugely frustrated, I paused and leaned on the edge of the bay to watch a young guy also on the range hitting each ball with what can only be described as something close to perfection. Awesomely smooth and powerful blasts. Time after time after time. His swing was hypnotic in its rhythm. It seemed so far removed from my own and the wee fella didn't look more than fourteen. I had no idea then that I was watching Rory McIlroy, who went on to smash the course record at Royal Portrush with an astonishing 61 in the summer of 2005. Rory's subsequent meteoric rise and the scope of his talent have left the establishment reeling.

After a good fifteen minutes of watching his swing, my frustration slowly turned to curiosity, then to awe, and gradually back to some self-belief. It's just a swing to hit a ball, I told myself. I can do it. How bloody hard can it be? So I went back to the task in hand, strangely elated, and proceeded to hit some of the best shots I'd ever hit in my life. Bizarrely, my huge slice and poor striking had turned into a tiny facsimile of what Rory was doing. Some of his rhythm, at the very least, had filtered into my swing, and my striking was infinitely better as a result.

This subconscious absorption of a perfect swing seemed to tie in with Jim's teaching and now I felt that I was really onto something. It is true that the mechanics always will be important and a poor grip or set-up will mess up even the best swing, but clearly it was possible to strike the club better without having to know every single detail of where your hands and legs should be throughout the swing.

Fired up by my discovery, I downloaded a snippet of Jim's swing and set it on a loop on my computers at home and at work. I would watch it over and over again until I could feel myself absorbing it. It became a ritual for me – morning, noon and night. Debbie lent me a child's seven iron and I stood in front of my computer at home, swinging in the same rhythm as Jim. At work most of our meetings were held in my office, which allowed me to sit behind my desk and play the big boss, with Jim swinging away on the computer screen in front of me. Hopefully (but realistically, doubtfully), I was concentrating on work, but I was hoping, too, that at some subconscious level Jim's swing was filtering deep down into my soul.

I bought a mobile phone with a video player and recorded Jim's swing onto its tiny screen. I would set it to a four-minute loop and then place it in the phone holder on the dashboard of my car. Whenever I was stuck in traffic, I'd let it run and run, until the exasperated hooting of the car behind would break my trance.

At the range I was hitting the ball better and I started to play around to test the concept. I'd warm up and then hit ten balls with my six iron. I'd gauge roughly how well and accurately they had been struck. I'd watch Jim's swing for a minute on my phone or laptop and then try again. And each time there'd be a marked improvement. It would hardly stand up as a statistically valid piece of research, but I definitely struck the ball better after I watched the video.

I was, of course, still taking weekly half-hour lessons with Debbie. Her simple and uncomplicated approach to teaching golf kept me straight. Her temperament is measured and calm – an excellent foil to my regular overexcitability. I'd come bouncing along like Tigger, full of enthusiasm about something I'd read or done and the big change it was going to make. She'd nod her head in an indulgent fashion and get me to strike a few balls. Then she would simply point out my errors – my swing plane was wrong, or my grip was still off – and in ten shots she'd have me back on track.

During these lessons we had some fascinating conversations about how people learn, and the difficulties of teaching such a complex set of movements without moving into overload.

'Have you ever been to a wedding where they do that organised céilidh dancing?' I asked her one day.

'No, but I think I know the sort of thing you mean,' Debbie answered, with a puzzled look that told me she was wondering just where exactly I was taking the conversation.

'Well, not to put too fine a point on it, I'm absolutely bloody useless at it. They have callers, standing on the stage with the musicians, to teach you the dances. They tell you to put a foot here, a hand there, twist, turn, move both feet, blah, blah, blah, and then expect that with one walk-through you're going to remember it. The amazing thing is that some people do remember it.'

'Right,' she said, looking blankly at me.

'What I'm saying is that my brain doesn't work that way. I'm utterly useless at it. I need to see something over and over again before I can grasp it. Explain it to me just one time, however logically, and my brain fogs over.'

'Actually, I do know what you mean,' Debbie said, her face brightening. 'It's the YMCA-dance syndrome. Some guy tells you to move your hands like this and like that for each letter, and by ...'

'... the time you get to C you're totally lost,' we both chimed together, delighted to have found common ground.

'That's it exactly,' I said. 'I mean, how hard can it be to learn four bloody letters that you make with your hands? And yet I always get it mixed up. I know that if I could just watch the sequence about ten times in a row, I'd get it right, but when it's broken down into its parts it loses the flow.'

'Yep – me too,' laughed Debbie. 'I completely get your point.'

Bizarre as it may seem, this analogy proved to be very useful for me throughout the year. There clearly are many different ways to learn golf and I do wonder if much of the way it is traditionally taught isn't inherently flawed. But undoubtedly the presence of a good teaching professional is hugely important. There are some basic fundamentals that you just can't ignore and a lot of the so-called quick fixes and add-an-extra-30-yards-to-your-drive courses do more harm than good.

My initial goal had been to do my control round and then not play again for at least a month to get my basic swing right. I hoped that I'd be able to make a major leap within this first period to get me up and running. The plan was to follow a score path something like this:

    May – 103
    June – 90
    July – 85
    August – 82
    September – 80
    October – 78

November – 77
December – 76
January – 75
February – 74
March – 73
April – 72
May – 71

This plan was ridiculed by some people on the Internet bulletin board but I felt I needed some interim targets to aim for. It's universally acknowledged within the game that taking ten shots off a 100-shooter is much easier than taking half as many shots off an 80-shooter. I had, albeit more than twenty years previously, been a 90-shooter, so it seemed plausible in my optimistic head that I could be shooting a 90 again within a month or so. With the seasonal good weather and lots of time to play, I hoped that I could easily get this to an 85 within another month. After that, it was little more than drawing a relatively straight line all the way to a nice shiny 71 next May.

I knew that winter would be tough and the nagging feeling never left me that it had been very foolish to change from the original plan of starting in September. As it turned out, I had absolutely no idea of just how tough it would be to keep that rate of improvement going through the dark winter months. When I looked at the figures at the start of the challenge, it seemed that the score of 78 by October would be the hardest to attain. I was aiming to take off twenty-five shots within six months and that seemed a very tall order indeed.

Obsession and Some Harsh Realities

Success consists of going from failure to failure
without loss of enthusiasm.

WINSTON CHURCHILL

By mid-June I was going at it like a man possessed and, in spite
of my promises to myself and to Lesley, the challenge was
starting to impact on my work and home life. I was using every
available opportunity to practise and immerse myself in golf. It
wasn't causing any specific problems in either environment just
yet but there's no doubt it was taking up more time than I first
thought it would. This relentless practising was beginning to
concern Debbie, though.

Practising on hard range mats is tough on the joints generally
and on the wrists in particular. At Blackwood the facilities for
practice centre around a fantastic driving range but no area to
practise off grass. This meant that the driving-range mats were
where the majority of my efforts were directed. My arthritic hips
were holding up fine most of the time but I was getting a lot of
pain in my right wrist, caused by the constant jarring of the club
against the mat. Debbie was aware of this and kept warning me
to go easy. But going easy at this stage would have put the
project in jeopardy, and I felt I had no choice in the matter.

As well as being the chief teaching professional, Debbie also
pretty much manages the centre, so she is there a huge amount

of time. She always knew when I was there and just how much practice I was putting in. In the early stages she talked about giving me a couple of range tokens each week and then checking them off to ensure I had been doing enough practice. Very quickly she realised, however, that the problem lay in trying to stop me practising too much. I used to nip out of work for an hour or so at lunch and then be back again for at least an hour in the evening after doing my dutiful family things. When my wrists became painful, she was concerned. I felt that I had to keep at it while the momentum was spurring me on. But having once, at the height of her career, over-practised to a point where she ended up on a surgeon's table with a subsequent six-month lay-off with her wrist in a cast, Debbie was worried that I might jeopardise the project before we'd got it off the ground.

She encouraged me to practise only once a day, and to take a few days off now and then to rest my wrists and get a bit of perspective. Unfortunately, by this stage I was totally addicted. Living, breathing, sleeping and eating golf. Outside of work, if I wasn't at the range, I was reading golf books or watching golf videos and planning my next trip to the range. I continued to take every available opportunity to swing clubs at home, both outside and inside the house.

My behaviour, in fact, was becoming faintly ridiculous. I would drive up to the range and hide my car at the far end of the car park, sneaking about like someone with a drug or alcohol dependency. With the parking area obscured by trees, Debbie couldn't see my car from the office or reception and I would creep out to a practice bay that couldn't be easily seen from most other areas. If she was teaching, then I'd be caught out, but I often managed to get away with it. I never actually lied to her when she congratulated me on taking things a bit easier, but I certainly didn't put her straight either.

In retrospect it was bizarre behaviour but this is what a challenge can do to you. It also highlights just how easy it is to become addicted to golf per se. I'm not the first person to succumb to its spell and I won't be the last. It has an amazing ability to dominate totally the lives and thinking of otherwise sane men and women.

Debbie's concerns were well founded. I did reach a stage where I was suffering constant pain in my right wrist and shouldn't have been practising at all. To combat the pain I began to practise a one-armed stroke, which turned out to be a blessing in disguise. It taught me how to swing with much greater ease and rhythm instead of bashing the ball all the time. I would go through a routine with my left arm and then do some very gentle pitches with both arms. As long as I kept it very soft, I could manage it. It was a godsend. My wedge play improved enormously during this period partly because I was unable to concentrate on anything else.

This left-arm-only method formed a strong part of my practice ritual throughout the year. John Daly, the maverick US golfer more famed for his booming drives, uses a similar method and believes that it has transformed his own short game. So I felt encouraged that I was doing something useful while trying to work around my injury.

And then, several weeks into the challenge and nearing the end of June, I felt ready to get back out there and test myself. I had worked incredibly hard and needed to see what progress I had made.

Full of confidence with my improved swing, I played six holes on my own. My efforts, however, merely resulted in a devastating bogey, double bogey, bogey, double bogey. I sat on the tee at the fifth hole and could have cried. I was six over par after four holes. The challenge seemed utterly impossible. My putting was totally useless on the wet surface and my once-confident pitching and chipping had deteriorated now that I'd moved away from the range and the security of the practice area.

I had a quiet chat with myself and tried to pull it together. My mind was a whirl of all the comments, good and bad, I had received in the past few weeks. Here I was, out on my own, less than two months into the challenge, already breaking down with the pressure of it all. And the pressure was intolerable, especially as I had stuck my neck out by telling even more people what I was planning to do. I had to calm down and accept that there was a long way to go. This pressure and the need to deal with it would become a major factor throughout the year.

But that day, with some perspective and rational thinking, I did pull myself together. Although I bogeyed the next two holes, I knew that I'd actually played them well and was unlucky not to hole putts for par on both. I'd played four shots better on those holes than I had on my original round. There had clearly been some progress. This experience highlighted just how different a range game is to striking the ball on the course.

I continued to practise alone and I played a few nine-hole sessions in the evening with mixed results. My play was definitely improving, although my putting remained very poor. This didn't overly concern me because I knew that I couldn't change everything in one go. The putting could wait until the winter months (or so I told myself). With a discernible improvement in all other aspects of my game, and with a strong feeling of confidence, in the first week of July I organised a game with my father at my old club in Portstewart.

This small northern town, as I said earlier, holds a unique and very strong attraction for me. It has two golf courses – a par-64 course on one side of town and the relatively famous par-72 Strand course on the other. The wee course, as we used to call it, was where we played as kids. It's very short and has no par-five holes. Much of the back nine involves some very short par fours with little or no trouble, providing excellent scoring opportunities. It was at this course that I played in my early teens and got my handicap down to 15.

The Strand course is a different kettle of golfing fish altogether. Perched right on the beach and winding its way through the famous, tall sand hills, it is a proper test of anyone's game. Since I'd lived in Portstewart the course had received a huge makeover and was now even tougher and more intimidating on the first few holes. It was on this course that my father and I had agreed to play and it would provide a very suitable measure of how my golf would fare outside of the comfort zone of the range and pleasant evenings out on a relatively wind-free Blackwood.

It was important to me to let my father see my progress. No matter what age you are, you always want to impress your dad. I wanted to show him what a great a son he had and how easily I could have become that golf professional all those years ago.

The round, however, would be a brutal example of just how far I had yet to go. I knew that if I could shoot a 90 on this course, I would be deliriously happy with my progress. But I felt extremely intimidated as I stood on the front nine.

I went out in 62. A horrific score. I slogged along the sixth, seventh and eighth, desperate to impress my father, but my game just got worse and worse. I was a quivering wreck and played like someone with absolutely no ability whatsoever. I three-putted *every* green and lost five balls. I remember thinking that if I shot another 62 on the back nine, I'd shoot a 124, which would be 34 strokes away from my target and an astonishing 21 more than my control round at Blackwood a couple of months earlier.

Once more I felt like crying. This was the first real test in public of my progress and I was royally messing it up. I stood on the tenth tee and babbled all sorts of pathetic excuses about why I was doing so badly – I'm just not used to this course ... It's such a different game up here from what I've been used to at Blackwood ... The progress I've been making there is incredible ... It's a shame you haven't seen me play there. It all sounded weak and stupid. Golf is golf is golf and here I was playing golf at a level you'd expect from a total beginner. I despise puny excuses in my business life, yet here I was behaving like a work-shy employee offering different reasons for arriving in late every day. I wanted the ground to open up and swallow me *and* my stupid challenge.

My father kept playing calmly, trying to enjoy the day. He knew I was struggling and in a meltdown, but he tried to help me stay in control by not making a big issue out of it.

Not for the first time did I wonder just why on earth I had decided to do it this way. Why hadn't I just taken up golf again as a proper hobby like other sane people? I could have worked hard at it over a few years until I was content with a handicap of

11 or 12. It suddenly seemed utterly absurd, this thing that I was doing. This daft goal of mine, which nearly everyone was telling me wasn't possible, was ruining an otherwise perfect opportunity for a pleasant family occasion.

Obviously giving up and going home wasn't an option, so I had a stern chat with myself at the ninth and tried to start again. I hate self-pity even more than I hate excuses. I told myself to snap out of it and relax. The back nine at the Strand course is a fair bit easier and, therefore, a lot less intimidating. I tried to put some trust back into my swing, focusing on all the positive work I had been doing. I conjured up the image of the perfect swing. The result? I came back in 42, which included four holes at level par.

I hadn't three-putted at all on the back nine and by simply swinging smoothly and trusting my rhythm, it had all started to flow. Even so, the harsh reality was 104, one shot more than I had taken at my control round. I tried to console myself with the fact that the Strand is a par-72 course, while Blackwood is a par 71.

In an odd way, I regarded this as progress. Indeed, I found myself having to look at so many scores during the year as progress, even though the raw figures were so bad. It just shows how tough a game of golf can be when you are playing for a score and not points or match play. One bad hole can completely destroy your round in a way that can be avoided in many other forms of golf, particularly the Stableford points system. I also couldn't allow any gimmes on the green, which are taken for granted in normal friendly play.

The reality is that, although I played badly overall, I had actually shot a decent back nine. My front-nine performance was badly affected by my poor mental state. I knew when I started the challenge that control over the mental aspects of the game was going to be crucial. All golfers accept that the mental side of golf is vital but very few actually do anything about it. The key to my success had to be a very clear understanding of how to use my brain power to get me round the course, rather than just relentlessly pursuing the perfect swing on the range.

I continued to work hard over the next few days and played a few more holes in the evenings with reasonable results. Debbie felt that my progress was good and that I needn't worry too much about my putting even though it continued to be very poor. She was firmly of the opinion that we couldn't do everything at once and that while a year was, in terms of the overall challenge, a short period of time, it was still long enough to enable me to break down the various aspects of the game into different stages.

When I did have my first putting lesson, Debbie noticed that I was making a stabbing motion at the ball rather than a nice fluid acceleration through it. A cardinal error, shared by so many golfers. I was tending to take a long backswing and then slowing down through the ball, with predictably disastrous results. I was still capable of four-putting, which I absolutely had to stop.

Another problem, and one that still plagues me to this day, is that, at heart, I'm a macho golfer. My tendency is to 'under club' and try to murder the ball to the green. If the choice is a gentle seven iron or a hard eight, I'll always go for the eight, with the result that, even with an excellent shot, I'm very often short of the green. I realised that I needed to work just as hard on my course management as on other aspects of my game.

Settling into a Rhythm

Genius is one per cent inspiration and ninety-nine
per cent perspiration.

THOMAS ALVA EDISON

As the year progressed, it soon became clear just how difficult the
challenge was going to be in terms of 'balance'. It seemed that
it wasn't quite as easy to slot in the various demands of my em-
ployees and fellow directors and my family life as I had imagined.
I was generally coping well, but my relentless focus on golf was
spilling over into both my work and family life. This was something I needed to be careful of.

I hadn't reached the stage where I was missing family events
or forgetting about business meetings, but I wasn't far off it. My
lunch-time practice sessions were stretching more into the
working day than was strictly professional and I was starting to
feel guilty every evening when I left Lesley at home with the
ironing and the television, and Aimee.

My daily routine involved taking Aimee to school and then going
to my office at our main garden centre in Donaghadee. At lunch
time I would drive the fifteen minutes to Blackwood and hit the
range for half an hour or so, and return to the garden centre and
work until about six or seven o'clock. Then it was home for dinner,
play with Aimee and story time. By eight-thirty I was leaving the
house again and heading back to the range, about ten minutes' drive
away. There's no doubt about it – it was a hugely selfish challenge.

I've never had any interest in team sports, and at school would almost sulk round a rugby pitch, getting indignant when somebody on the team told me what to do. Later, I joined the school rowing club, but again had very little interest in bothering to put any real effort into it. Golf appealed to me enormously, in the same way that skiing does, because, on any given day, you're out there on your own, just you and the elements. There's no one else to let you down, or for you to let down.

I had begun to enjoy the calm and almost Zen-like state that comes with long sessions at the range. Initially, several hours there seemed like a huge slog but now it was becoming a great pleasure. I can see how the Singhs of this world can practise for such vast periods of time. You reach a wonderful state of calm, mixed with intense pleasure. The best times were when I was alone at the range late in the evening. Other golfers would be sitting at home watching television or having a drink in the pub. But here was I getting better *and* enjoying myself at least every bit as much as they were, which was particularly satisfying when I thought of those golfers who doubted my success. This sense of competition against the nay-sayers was a very useful motivating tool and served me well throughout the year.

Around this time I read *Mastery* by George Leonard, a book aimed at the martial arts and aikido community, extolling the joys of the daily repetition of simple tasks. The same principles seemed to be working for me and my golf. Practice came to be something I relished, rather than dreaded, and I eagerly looked forward to my daily visits to Blackwood.

The downside, however, was that I'd become a little too addicted to the sterile world of range practice. At many stages during the year, a little more time actually playing golf would have revealed more clearly what I was doing well or badly. But it was all too easy to come up with excuses not to play six holes, always easier just to toddle off to the range. Wasn't there always a scramble to find a slot on the course? What about the threat of rain? There were many excuses and each one saved me from facing the truth – that I found the course too intimidating. That's where it could all go wrong. So the range quickly became my comfort zone. I was safe there and could play with the variables without having to face up to the reality of a score.

Nevertheless, when I did manage to get out, I continued to see some decent progress. As ever, though, there were huge swings in my scoring. But playing alone at Blackwood meant that I was once again putting myself in a fairly sterile and unrealistic environment. At some stage, and the sooner the better, I needed to perform with some level of skill in front of other golfers. Still, it kept the pressure to a minimum and saved me from getting too discouraged with bad rounds being witnessed by others.

In the middle of July I slipped out in the last hour or so of light when there was practically nobody on the course. Playing an empty, or nearly empty course, is still something I love. It's akin to taking the last ski lift up a mountain when everyone else has decided to pack up for the day – a delight that my brother Patrick and I relished when we went skiing together. The après-ski bars would be full and there we would be, just us two, standing at the summit. We'd wait for the lifts to stop and then journey down – an exquisite and silent pleasure. On this particular evening at Blackwood, I experienced a similar feeling and my playing was relaxed and hugely enjoyable.

Two pars at the opening two holes greatly helped my mood, but I followed up with a less than grand three putts and a double bogey at the tricky par-three third hole. My confidence was not overly dented, however, and my play over the next three holes went par, bogey, par, par and birdie. Since the course was so empty, I cut across to the eighteenth tee. I stood there at two over par for eight holes, euphoric at my progress. So much so that, even at that late hour, I texted Patrick, my sister Katriona and Debbie to give them the great news.

From the moment I told them about the challenge, Patrick and Katriona had been very supportive. Patrick had moved back to Northern Ireland a few years after my return from university and was happily married and living in Portstewart. He had lost all interest in golf after his teens. In our younger days, the bug had never really bitten him as deeply as it had me. Katriona, an occupational therapist, was living in New York. They both knew only too well how much golf had meant to me in the past and they shared my enthusiasm for getting stuck in to new adventures. I phoned them many times during the year and got a lot of support and encouragement when things weren't going well. As I stood there on my own that night at Blackwood I wanted to share the moment with them. They texted back, genuinely delighted with my progress.

The light had almost completely gone by now but I thought I'd play back down the eighteenth anyway. I drove and immediately lost sight of my ball but wandered off in the vague direction that I thought it had gone. I found it relatively easily and bashed it up in the darkness towards the green. I found it again and ended up with a bogey.

So I was three over par for nine holes, with one hole played in total darkness. I'd always had a strong belief that I could win the challenge, but here, once and for all, was the proof. I knew that for all my ups and downs, so far I'd been doing the right things. A wave of positive emotion swept over me, wiping out my recent Portstewart humiliation and all the pain of the practice in one fell swoop. In just a couple of months I was showing an enormous, quantifiable level of improvement, which filled me with a renewed sense of optimism and motivation.

Much of the key to my progress was down to the huge number of balls I had hit with my wedge when my wrist was so bad. Those one-handed pitches had improved my confidence immensely. Having all sorts of daft notions now that I could maybe even complete the goal within six months, I hit the range the next night ... and suffered a total meltdown. Horrific slices, hooks and even shanking with my wedges. And there is no more brutal a sound in golf than that of the shank.

It never ceases to amaze me how golf can bring you to euphoric highs one minute and viciously boot you the next, taking the wind from your sails. This pattern would last the year out. Every time my spirits plummeted and I thought I couldn't go on, the golfing gods would give me a break and I'd have a good round to spur on my motivation. However, the second I even thought about getting above myself, they would blast me back to reality.

For me, these golfing gods are the great past masters of the art. In his seminal book on achievement, *Think and Grow Rich!*, Napoleon Hill talks about the power of using a mastermind group in both a real and an imaginary sense. He would imagine himself sitting in a room discussing his problems with some of history's great achievers, like Henry Ford or Thomas Edison. For someone with an imagination as fertile as mine, this is a great concept and one that I'd used in the past. I'd been a car and motor-racing fanatic and had even bought a silly fast car and taken part in a number of track days at local racing circuits. It was the type of sport that appealed to me, since it was essentially a solitary activity, but it is always useful to have a bit of help. So, driving at these events, I would have the legendary Ayrton Senna sitting beside me, offering advice and keeping me calm. (He had his work cut out on that score, clearly.) Having an imaginary Ayrton in my car used to cause great hilarity amongst my track-day friends, but it's a psychological trick that can be tremend-ously powerful. Fundamentally, all it does is help you tap into your own common sense. When you're in the middle of a problem, it can be difficult to view it objectively. This technique allows you to stand outside yourself and view a challenge or problem from a different perspective.

Ayrton, of course, was no use when it came to playing golf. Tutting and mumbling 'Just go faster' in an exasperated Brazilian fashion obviously wasn't going to help my putting. With this challenge I needed a different kind of expert. After some con-sideration, I narrowed the choice down to Seve Ballesteros or Ben Hogan. But in the end, for me there was only one person who could fill Ayrton's shoes as my swashbuckling mentor. Thinking back to the way the hair on the back of my neck stood on end that day in Dublin when he walked on to the tee, it could only be Seve.

For the duration of my challenge, this would prove to be a tremendously important and stimulating relationship. I'd drive along in my car or stand at the range and have profound conversations with Seve about my game, and he'd help me put any of my problems into perspective. Occasionally, I'd have Hogan piping up from the back seat to offer advice about practice, but most of the time it was just me and Seve.

I would go so far as to say that without Seve's help, especially with my short game, I simply wouldn't have made it. Of course I did make a fool of myself on more than one occasion at the range, nodding and saying 'I know, I know' to an empty bay when Seve had chastised me for doing something stupid. All I could do was offer a simpering smile to any golfer who had overheard me. They must have thought I was barking.

I still had a lot of learning to do about the nature of golf and what a cruel game it can be, but having Seve around me helped enormously. When things went wrong, it felt good to have him sitting in the car beside me, conducting the all-important postmortems. He was always there, talking away in that smooth Spanish accent, demanding my attention. And I never regretted one of those imaginary conversations – without fail, they always helped me to look at the positive side of things and feel better about fighting another day.

During the school holidays, Lesley, Aimee and I spent a week in Portstewart at my parents' house. It gave us all a bit of a break from my relentless practising and the chance to spend some time together.

I was also hoping to fit in a couple of rounds at the local course. The best way to do this, without annoying Lesley too much, was to get up at the crack of dawn and be back by ten o'clock or so; then spend the rest of the day with the family. On the first morning I got to the small, 64-par course around half past six and there wasn't a soul about, which suited me very well. When I played on my own during this period I carried my bag and moved around the course rapidly in an effort to improve my fitness. I had to get fitter during the challenge but gym time was a luxury I couldn't afford. So, like a madman, I'd basically run round the course carrying the bag and doing lifts with it to improve my arm strength. This was fine on an empty course with no one in front, but with other golfers about, my lightning fast rounds could easily be extended by an hour or so, which would eat into work or home time.

That morning I played fairly well and shot twelve over par for the eighteen. The following morning I arrived at the same time but was irritated to find people already on the course. So I ran like an idiot up the first tee and started at the second to get ahead of them. Flustered by my impatience and the rush, I hit a bad tee shot and gradually descended into golf hell, hacking my way across the first few holes. The green-keepers were out in force, too, and I got a chewing from one old boy on the sixth green for being out so early. I felt like a fourteen-year-old school kid again. Standing on the seventh tee, fresh from a bollocking, I wondered again what it was that was possessing me to do this. Lesley and Aimee were snugly tucked up in bed and I was out here playing bad golf and getting shouted at into the bargain. It was clearly time to go home. I shoved the driver back in my bag and scuttled down the road to my car.

I decided, wisely I think, to give golf up for the rest of the week. Although the weather wasn't brilliant, we had a great time and it was a huge relief to be freed up from the madness of the project for a few days. We went to the beach, and sat on the promenade eating ice cream in the rain. In the evenings we ate out a lot and drank too much red wine. I made up stories for Aimee and just played being dad without having to over-compensate for my absences. I may have flicked through a couple of golf magazines but that was the height of it – there was no putting on the carpet, no swinging fictional clubs in the mirror and no visualising the perfect round at every available quiet moment. For a few days at least it was peace and relaxation. I think Lesley even started to like me again.

'Dick!'

Experience is simply the name we give our
mistakes.

OSCAR WILDE

Our house looked like a bomb site. My books and videos lay
about everywhere. I had generally three golf books on the go at
any one time, as well as all the major golf magazines (about six
a month). I was also receiving a lot of advice from the folk on
the Australian forum, where I was still blogging my progress. So
I was getting a lot of information every month, much of it
conflicting.

During a fascinating conversation, a writer for one of the magazines told me that they regularly had conflicting pieces of advice
within the same issue. You would find a cure for the slice on
page 58, for example, which directly conflicted with advice on
page 134. Both pieces of advice might come from highly
respected teachers. Who was to say which was right and which
was wrong? All the editors in the magazine could do was make
sure the articles were located as far apart as possible, and hope
that not too many readers noticed.

My relentless search for an easy answer and instant gratification meant that on many occasions I ignored the simple and sage
advice that Debbie was giving me. My persistent searching
wasn't helped by the fact that, in Jim McLellan's method, I felt
I'd discovered a secret. I was still spending a huge amount of

time watching perfect swings and trying to absorb the movement into my own swing. I had proved, without a shadow of a doubt to myself at least, that this worked. Standing at the range, I'd hit twenty shots with my driver and make a judgement as to the 'score' based on a relatively arbitrary measure of what I thought was an excellent drive. For five minutes or so, I'd watch Jim's swing, or one or two other excellent swings I had on my mobile. Then I'd hit another twenty shots. In every case, without fail, my score would be better. This breakthrough convinced me that there were more 'secrets' to be learned. Secrets that could, at the very least, complement the lessons of a good teaching pro.

At this stage my lessons with Debbie were becoming much less frequent. We had been through the basics and it was now up to me to keep at it until it became second nature. A combination of my holidays, Debbie's holidays and Debbie becoming extremely busy meant that I went through an eight-week period with only one lesson. This was far too long a break from her steadying hand and it set me off, like a fool, looking for answers and those elusive secrets elsewhere.

On the recommendation of several folk on the forum I bought *Tour Tempo* by John Novosel, which was pitched, like so many other books and products, as 'Golf's final secret revealed'. What I was after was some sort of process to keep my range work more consistent and to help me transfer my practice to the course more effectively.

In *Tour Tempo* Novosel outlines a process designed to improve the tempo of your swing, in line with the tempo of the professionals. It was observed that no matter how fast the pros swing, the relationship between the speed of the backswing and the downswing remained the same. A CD-ROM accompanied the book to help amateurs achieve this tempo, thereby improving their game.

The concept sounded good, so I gave it a shot for a few weeks. I found that, while the process may work for some people, for me it proved to be a disaster. I was trying to fix a part of my swing that didn't need fixing. As a result, I started to make a complete mess of my game, culminating in a bad session at Blackwood.

I was on the tee around seven in the morning to get nine holes in before work. It went spectacularly wrong. With a vicious slice, I sent my tee shot straight into the trees. I calmly reloaded and this time hooked the ball so badly that it disappeared into rough on the other side of the fairway, never to be seen again. Mildly disconcerted, I tried again, only to slice two more tee shots off into the trees. I'd lost four balls and I hadn't even made it off the first tee. Totally spooked, I shoved the driver back in my bag and trudged the lonely walk of a beaten man back to my car. It wasn't going to be my day.

Here was an obvious lesson in how not to over-complicate things. I'd been trying too hard and ignoring the fundamentals. As I walked back to the car, I could sense Seve walking behind me. He just followed and stayed silent. I ignored him – I knew what was coming. A long and passionate dissertation as to how stupid I had been and how important it was to avoid the type of revelation to be found in books like *Tour Tempo*. How I needed to get out there and learn by myself. That some stupid timing trick was never going to help. I slowly packed my clubs in the car and prepared myself for the lecture.

He sat down beside me and I thought it best to get it over with before we drove off. I looked at him and said, 'I know, I know – I know exactly what you're going to say.'

He scowled at me with a look of utter disdain and after what seemed like an eternity he opened his mouth and muttered: 'Meester Richardson. You are a dick!'

With that, he calmly opened the door, got out of the car, and left me to lick my wounds.

He was right, of course. No more needed to be said on the subject. I was a dick.

As if it didn't need to be rammed home to me how stupid I'd been, a few days later Debbie passed me on the range and, without even stopping, cheerily said, 'Too high, Johnnie Boy.' A reference to the position of my hands on the club and a problem I had been having at our last lesson. Within minutes, I was hitting the ball beautifully again and almost crying with relief. I've said it before and no doubt will say it again, but a good pro who keeps it simple and knows your swing is worth her weight in gold. It's just a shame that I ignored my own advice too often.

Many people have said to me that if they had unlimited access to lessons, then they, too, could make huge improvements. But this is an overly simplistic view. The average amateur simply needs to take a few lessons on a regular basis and then practise, with some diligence, what they have been taught. It's extremely difficult to learn the swing from a book or video, and the average cost of a lesson is so little in comparison to the price of a new driver, or even a meal at the club, that it just doesn't make sense not to make use of them. Professional trainers see so many swings every week that it takes them only a few seconds to diagnose a problem and give you a solution. This knowledge is gold dust and, as I say, relatively inexpensive. Working the solution through is, however, up to you. What a pro cannot do is make you practise.

I continued to make breakthroughs and did discover more secrets of the game, but the priority now was getting back to the basics and making sure my fundamentals were correct. The one common strand that flows through all the major instructional manuals is an adherence to the basics – grip, stance, alignment, posture and so on. Get yourself in a good position to begin with and take the club straight back on the right path and you're most of the way there. I'd managed to mess a lot of this up by making it all too complicated, so when I finally got my next lesson scheduled with Debbie, we felt it was time to get out the video camera and have a good look at what was going on.

It was now four months into the challenge and my grip still wasn't right, so Debbie lent me a specially formed grip that forced my hands into position. As I sat at my desk, watched television or talked on the phone, I held this thing, trying to force my brain to remember once and for all the position my hands needed to stay in. I also reread Hogan's *Five Lessons: The Modern Fundamentals of Golf* and scanned his grip picture into my PC as my desktop wallpaper. So, in the idle moments when I wasn't watching Jim's swing, I could concentrate on Hogan's grip and drill that image into my head.

Over the next few weeks I recommitted to some very hard graft and made excellent progress. I'd be lying if I said that I ignored all other information, but I'd learned a lesson – I stuck to the basics and began to reap rewards using this simple approach.

I played a round with my brother-in-law, Paul, who has been a committed golfer for most of his adult life. At this stage his handicap had drifted up to 14 from a peak of 11. I had played with him a couple of times in the previous ten years, so he was familiar with my game, and would inevitably thrash me. This time, however, I played well – so well, in fact, that I beat him. Needless to say, he was impressed by my progress.

That night Lesley was on the phone with her sister Karalyn (Paul's wife). When the call was over, she told me that Paul had been amazed by my progress. A little bit of praise goes a long way and suddenly it all seemed to be possible again. I had turned another small corner in the process.

In the first week of September my sister got married and the wedding was held in Portstewart. Katriona's husband-to-be was from Scotland, so we had a huge entourage of Scots and Americans coming over for the big day and had planned some good, old-fashioned Northern Irish hospitality. The reception was held in the golf clubhouse in the town and memorably we all stood together at the end of the day and watched as the sun drifted down over the vast sand hills that surround the course. An incredible sunset, which reaffirmed to me just how wonderful a sport golf can be if you can allow yourself to appreciate the beautiful settings of most courses.

A big game organised for the wedding guests meant another opportunity to test out my golf at the Strand course – the scene of my nightmarish 104 just a few months earlier. The wind howled and the rain lashed like it only can at the very best Scottish and Irish links courses, and the sight of visiting Americans braving these conditions was a bonus. I expected them to be horrified by the atrocious weather but such is the romantic draw of links golf in Scotland and Ireland that they loved it.

My game wasn't too bad. I concentrated hard on my course

management and, with the help of Seve, shot a 90. (Seve was wearing his St Andrews 1984 outfit in recognition of the links setting, and throughout the round he uttered a few timely remarks about altering my game to suit the conditions.) Not what my target should have been at that stage, but a good score given the weather, and with some excellent golf again on the back nine holes.

I was seeing progress on the course, as a result of my swing and range work, but I was ignoring the short game. All golfers know that it is the short game, as well as the mental game, that really helps the scores, yet it seems to be a fundamental part of their psyche to stand at the range and bash the drives rather than practise this vital element. I had promised myself at the beginning of the challenge that I wouldn't let this happen, but I fell into the trap time and time again.

A rumbling of criticism could be heard from my distant Australian friends about this lack of emphasis, but buoyed up by my improvement, I chose to ignore it. After all, what did they know?

The Relentless March of Technology

I dream, I test my dreams against my beliefs, I dare
to take risks, and I execute my vision to make
those dreams come true.

WALT DISNEY

One of the promises I'd made to myself that I did keep was to resist the lure of technology for the first few months and the idea that brilliant equipment could make me a scratch player. The intervening twenty years since I'd played regularly had provided golfers with a huge array of new ways to spend their money. Every single aspect of the clubs now being used seemed to have changed and, it has to be said, generally for the better. Friends had been keen to let me try out their new clubs, and the drivers, in particular, had shown me just how much easier they made it to hit the ball. But I felt that to become embroiled in using different types of club too early in the challenge would confuse the work I was doing with my swing. The newfangled equipment could come later when I'd proved myself.

With some sense of satisfaction I kept bashing away with my ancient Mizuno irons, which were a hand-me-down from my father-in-law, an original Callaway Big Bertha and a £10 Mizuno three wood that dated back about fifteen years. My golf bag even boasted a couple of Dunlop 65s. If the old technology was good enough for the old guys, then it had to be good enough for me, at least until I got some swing basics together. A poor swing wasn't going to get any better with a £300 driver.

Seve would watch approvingly as I dragged out the old clubs. He would remind me how he had created his game out of one club – a three iron – and that, ultimately, golf was about skill and not the clubs. I sensed I was beginning to earn his respect and that maybe he'd use his influence with the other golfing gods and they'd give me a break later when I really needed it.

By September, then, with a few good rounds behind me and a half-decent swing, I started the process of looking at clubs that might help me hit the ball a little better. Wary as I'd been of taking these steps, I gradually changed my view about the modern equipment and just how much of a difference it can make. It may be true that great equipment will never make a bad golfer good, but good clubs, suited to your particular style, can certainly make a big difference in terms of consistency and confidence. Driver technology, in particular, had come on in leaps and bounds.

There is no pro shop at Blackwood, so I visited Colin Murphy, who ran the local Golf Spot. Colin was a scratch golfer and I hoped he could help me find my way through the bewildering range of clubs on the market. I had hit a few different clubs already and had a vague idea of what I liked, so I headed to the range with a selection of six irons. Mizuno MX23s and MP30s, Callaway X16s and a couple of Titliests made up the selection. Very quickly I settled on the Mizunos. The feel of these clubs was exceptional and, in particular, I fell in love with the rather expensive MP30s, which are a cross between a cavity-back and a blade-style club. The cavity-back iron is much easier to hit, whereas the blade style offers more feel and potentially a better ability to shape the ball.

At the range I seemed unable to miss-hit the MP30s and, despite the cost, I decided that these were the clubs for me. Once more, though, I nearly got caught out by the rarefied, or should I say, illusionary, atmosphere of the driving range. When I played golf on the course, I noticed a big difference in confidence between the cavity-back style MX23s and the MP30s. An article by Lee Westwood explaining how, even at his level, he prefers the easiest-to-hit clubs persuaded me to review my choice. Debbie was also very firmly in this camp.

So, with my confidence on the course as fragile as it was, I began to think that the best route was to get the MX23s. However, further digging around revealed that, although they provide a beautiful feel, Mizuno forged irons such as the MX23 and MP30 range are more likely to wear out on the face of the clubs. With me hitting up to four hundred balls a day on occasion, the last thing I wanted to do was spend £600 and then have to replace the clubs in six months. Some golfers suggested that I try the similar but non-forged MX15 irons, and a visit to eBay revealed that these were a lot cheaper, too. About to be discontinued and replaced with the MX17, a few sets were still available. For £200 I could have a brand new set of irons that were widely regarded as being one of the easiest-to-hit irons in their day. This was my first real foray into the addictive world of eBay and I soon discovered that for anyone with an obsessive nature, eBay is a dangerous place. My pompous spoutings about not spending money on equipment soon went out the window.

Initially, I thought I'd made a big mistake trading on eBay, because my MX15s got lost in the post. Standard Internet paranoia set in and I assumed I'd never see my money again. However, it turned out I was dealing with an excellent trader. They had no MX15s left but they sent me a brand new set of the just-launched MX17s for the same price. This was a genuine bargain, since the set was worth at least £350.

When the irons arrived, I was delighted. They made it a *lot* easier for me to strike the ball confidently. But my good trading experience made me a little too comfortable about buying stuff on eBay. Over the next few weeks I bought a variety of clubs on eBay and from Colin at Golf Spot. It worked out all right for me but I should add a word of warning: buying clubs can be a minefield and without decent facilities to try them out, you can end up making some pretty expensive mistakes.

My bag ultimately ended up looking like this:

DRIVER: TaylorMade R580XD Stiff Shaft 9.5 degree.
This brought about a total transformation of my driving. A great deal easier to hit than my old Big Bertha and capable of giving me at least an extra 20 yards off the tee. My already high driving confidence went through the roof with this club.

THREE WOOD: Ping G2 15 degree.
It took me a long time to find something that I could hit better than my £10 Mizuno, but when I tried one of these I was amazed. Fantastic club and once more improved my confidence.

HYBRID: TaylorMade Rescue TP No. 2.
An eBay purchase that I initially hit very well but sub-sequently struggled with. This club had a stiff Fujikura shaft and introduced me to just how important (and incredibly confusing) shaft selection and technology can be.

IRONS: 3 PW Mizuno MX17 regular shaft.
No doubt about it – a very easy club to hit. Missing some of the feel of the forged Mizunos but for the level of golf I was playing, I honestly don't think I could have got a better set of irons.

WEDGES: 52/56/60 Ping Tour.
Again, these are just about the easiest wedges to play currently on the market. Once I fully grasped what I should be using them for, they made a noticeable improvement to my scoring.

PUTTER: Odyssey 2-ball; Odyssey White Hot No. 7.
At this stage the world had gone Odyssey-2-ball mad and I saw no reason not to join them. Some crafty photography from an eBay retailer and some over-zealous (i.e. daft and gullible) purchasing from me meant that I ended up with an Odyssey White Hot No. 7 and not the 2-ball at all. Keen to be a sheep, I went down to Golf Spot and bought the correct model before very quickly realising that I infinitely preferred the 'mistake' club I purchased on eBay. Once more, this showed just how much putting is about confidence and feel and not about the club.

When you consider how relatively simple golf used to be with an average bag containing three woods, eleven irons, of which two are wedges, and a putter, the range of new clubs that promise to make the whole thing easier is mind-boggling. It's also indicative of how much money is spent on golf.

Drivers, in particular, are very expensive and there is an astonishing number of high handicappers out there who are prepared to spend upwards of £300 every couple of years. Some even replace drivers annually in a vain attempt to improve their game. I know of a 24-handicapper who paid more than £400 for a brand new TaylorMade R7 with adjustable weights. He then proceeded to spend hours testing whether he should set it for draw or neutral. I watched him at the range taking appalling swipes at balls that successively disappeared in all directions, then mulling over a few grams of weight difference. The power of marketing is *huge* in golf.

Another problem for the golfer, but of enormous advantage for the club manufacturers, is the bizarre experience that is the 'honeymoon period', which we all seem to experience with any new driver. Such is the quality of most new clubs these days that the average golfer will play any new driver better than their existing one. A confidence comes with seeing that shiny new head, and with the couple of good reviews you've read, you concentrate just that bit harder and your self-belief increases when striking it. This very often results in some exceptionally well-struck shots, and the woeful notion that this club is the saviour of our current driving starts to form. Out comes the credit card, followed by the pleasant two-week honeymoon period. But the underlying problems have not gone away, and on a sticky day out on the course with a few bad putts behind you, your new-found confidence soon disappears and you're pretty much back to square one.

The power of marketing nearly won me over, too, and I was vaguely tempted by one of these new R7 drivers to avoid spending valuable time learning how to fade or draw the ball. This would be a painless way to create shots, I thought. A quick five-minute chat with Seve, however, showed me the error of my ways.

'Meester Richardson – you jus' learn to heet the ball straigh'. OK? Trust me – you heet it straigh' on the course and you shoot par. It ees simple. Stop all thees stupi' club-with-weights nonsense.'

Needless to say, and to the utter exasperation of the Spanish maestro, I managed to confuse things by trying too many of the other clubs that were available. And I did too much experimenting on the course with my new clubs. In particular, I wasted a lot of shots and time trying to make the lob wedge do a job that it isn't intended to do. As a result, I actually played worse golf for several rounds with my shiny new clubs than I had done before I got them.

Seve had a lot to say about the lob-wedge phenomenon. It has been a pet hate of his for years and he regards it as one of the problems with the modern game. He has even called for it to be banned, so my experimenting with it before I fully understood what it was useful for was always going to get me in trouble.

One wet day I was out on the course playing solo and experimenting with the lob wedge. Seve was standing by, watching closely. I was consistently leaving the ball short of the green and had just managed to send my approach shot to the sixth hole straight into the bunker before the green. Seve had been quiet and increasingly tense during the previous few holes but this was enough for him. He turned to me with an angry scowl on his face.

'Hey, hey, hey – you put that stupeed club down and let me show you sometheeng.'

He pulled out a rusty old three iron and played the most beautiful, soft, floating lob with it. He followed this with a wonderfully graceful running chip and a pitch with a little bit of check spin. He then wandered over to the bunker and executed a perfect sand shot. All using the three iron and all far better than I could do with any of my fancy new clubs.

He pointed to my lob wedge.

'Now, Meester Richardson, you put that stupeed club away and learn some feel. Learn how to play the shot properly before you use that nonsense. I can't believe you are being so stupeed.

You gotta learn to really feel these shots and then use the clubs.'

I nodded my head slowly, like a little scolded puppy.

'You people these days, you think all these clubs are a magic peell. Take one a day and all your golfing worries are over. Rubbish. Eet's just rubbish. You understan'? Eh?'

'Yes, Seve, I do. I was, er ... just trying to experiment ... to make it easier ...'

'That ees my point.' He sighed and shook his head. 'Short cuts won't make eet easier. Learn with the first club that comes to han' and learn the feel. Eet's no' an easy game. It requires work and effort.'

'OK, OK, OK,' I replied indignantly.

He wandered off tutting and muttering, leaving me feeling like a schoolboy. And, like any schoolboy, I still thought I knew better and had to learn the hard way that he was right. It was only after countless woeful shots left short or ribbed across the green with the lob wedge that I came to understand that it wasn't a magic pill. It was a great club, but the golfer needs excellent skills to get the most out of it. After a lot of practice, and much later in the year, I became very fond of the club, but it probably held me back more than it benefited me during the actual challenge.

This was another lesson in how we tend to make golf much more complicated than it actually is. The swing is indeed complicated but you can and must make it simple. Club technology is enormously complex but, likewise, it can also be made simple. The best advice is to get the easiest-to-hit irons and driver you can find, with a shaft matched to your swing speed. If you find that you struggle with the longer irons, then by all means use a hybrid club and get a couple of decent wedges that you feel comfortable with. Then just get out and practise. Get confident using them. Act like you are nine years old again and the clubs you have chosen are your favourite new toys at Christmas. Walk around the house holding them, getting familiar with the weights. That way you'll be comfortable with them on the course.

Around this time I began to think about my fitness and weight. I didn't want to waste a lot of time at the gym, so I rigged up some golf-specific exercising apparatus at home, designed to improve my strength. I took apart a cheap set of dumb-bells and strapped a weight onto the face of an old club I had lying about in the garage. At least as effective as this was my old sledgehammer which also lived in the garage. Slowly swinging the club or sledgehammer in my living-room gym proved to be very useful, not just for strength conditioning but also for grooving-in my swing. I bought an elastic exercise band and devised a sequence of exercises to focus on golf-specific muscles. As a result, I was able to raise my fitness level easily and cheaply, without wasting time away from the course.

I still avoided using a trolley to transport my bag around the course. This built up my stamina, and although the effort of carrying the bag may have affected my energy levels in the last few holes, at this early stage I felt sure that it would pay off later when I was playing more regularly. Darren Clarke had recently lost a lot of weight and said that the principal benefit was that he no longer felt tired playing the last holes, especially if he had to play more than eighteen holes in a day. If it was good enough for Darren, it was good enough for me.

Of course, all these clubs and training aids didn't arrive at the house unnoticed. If I was a more tidy person, I could perhaps have stored them away a little better. As it was, wherever you looked you'd see a clutter of clubs, videos, putting mats, books and, of course, the sledgehammer. Rather naively, I assumed Lesley wouldn't mind too much since it was all part of my grand challenge. I was wrong.

'Lesley, where have you put my sledgehammer? I left it just over by the TV,' I asked in a rather exasperated tone one night. Didn't she realise how much I needed it?

'I put it in the garage. Where else do you expect that I might put a sledgehammer?' she responded, with at least as much tone.

I could tell I'd touched a nerve but bumbled on regardless, secure in the knowledge that my challenge was the most important thing in our lives at the moment.

'Yeah, I know, but I really need it. Is it so difficult to leave it in the living room?'

'Well, John,' she responded clearly and very assertively, 'to be honest, yes.'

I knew I'd stepped too far but was powerless to stop her. I could see the floodgates slowly open.

'Every bloody day something new arrives,' she continued. 'A man arrives at the door – "Package for Mr Richardson, will you sign for it?" – and every day I dutifully sign, knowing full well that whatever it is will just clutter the place up even more.'

'Yeah, but at least most of the stuff is second-hand. I'm buying old videos for a pound or so on eBay,' I replied in a defensive tone. Not a good response, if I'm honest, and she knew it.

'It's not just the money, it's the endless mess. It's the balls under the sofa, that stupid putting mat cluttering up the kitchen floor, the piles of books beside the bed, the videos all over the place upstairs, the sledgehammer – a bloody sledgehammer! – beside the TV in the living room. And all those silly weighted clubs that you put together and then leave the tape lying around the kitchen. Shall I go on?'

No, please no, I thought. There's a hell of a lot more than that; she hadn't even seen the stuff I'd been getting delivered to my office at the garden centre. I needed to quit now while the going was still relatively good.

'I understand and I am sorry. I just get totally carried away. But I do kinda need to get it all to see what works. I'll sell it all afterwards.'

'I know, I know, and I think it's really great. Honestly. But can you just try and keep it a little bit under control? When you've used a club, put it away; when you've watched a video, put it back in its box and back on the shelf. Is that unreasonable?'

'No, sorry. Point one hundred per cent taken. I will try.'

'That's all I'm asking.'

I'd got off pretty lightly – no doubt about it. It had become so easy just to expect that Lesley would accept the whole thing as normal and not get annoyed about it in any way. To her great credit she generally did, but my expecting to use a sledgehammer in the living room on a daily basis was clearly a bridge too far. I can't think why.

Three Control Rounds to Get My Handicap

> If you think you can do a thing or think you can't
> do a thing, you're right.
>
> HENRY FORD

It was the first week of October and I had been mainly practising and playing on my own, developing my game without too much external influence. Very soon the bad weather would set in and the course would revert to its winter status. That would mean temporary greens and rubber tees, which wouldn't provide me with an accurate measure of the stage I was at. It was time to join the golf club itself and put three cards in for a handicap.

I had been playing well and believed that a handicap in the low teens, even 11 or 12, would accurately reflect my level. Such a handicap would show my supporters, and my doubters, how much I had progressed in just a few short months.

For my first round, I chose to enlist the help of some of the regular club guys who manage to play every day around ten o'clock. As I had to take time off work, I hoped, rather naively, that I'd be able to play my eighteen holes in less than four hours and get to the office in the afternoon. During the summer months I'd had plenty of practice working within this time-frame, sometimes even as little as two hours, with early-morning rounds or getting out around eight in the evening and trying to beat the fading light.

Although I dutifully arrived at ten o'clock, we had to wait for the stragglers and didn't get onto the course until eleven-thirty. I realised that expecting to get back to work for the afternoon was stupid. As it turned out, the round took us four and a half hours to complete.

I was in the middle of a messy dismissal of an employee, as well as trying to make some fundamental changes to one of our cafés, so this wasn't the best time to be absent from work. The last thing I should have been doing was waltzing round a golf course with my new buddies. These work issues were on my mind and I was tense the whole way round the course. That, coupled with a certain nervousness at playing a game with new partners and a certain type of goldfish-bowl mentality of being observed and trying to show how much I'd progressed, resulted in catastrophe. I played terrible golf. Really terrible. Humiliating, actually. The type of golf that, not for the first time and definitely not for the last, made me wonder why I had bothered to put so much pressure on myself.

As ever, my driving saved the day and at least helped to show my playing partners that I could swing well and hit the ball. Armed with my new, bouncy big TaylorMade, I hit countless 300-yard drives, only to waste the whole thing with some appalling short-game work. I was at the height of my confusion and overuse of the lob wedge and in denial of Seve's advice at this time. Feeling utterly crushed, I checked my score: 95. Ninety-bloody-five. Weeks and weeks of hard work to take eight shots off my game? With a familiar feeling of rising panic and a complete inability to think rationally, I went home to lick my wounds.

I had planned to play golf in the winter league to help sharpen my competitive spirit, but this experience put me off. I should probably have stuck to this plan, though. It would have helped me grasp the notion of playing in a variety of different situations, which would undoubtedly have eased some of my mental fortitude problems in the latter stages.

A long, whiney, it's-so-hard chat with Debbie put things into perspective and she volunteered to come out with me and mark a card for my next round later that week. This would help me to calm down, since I had nothing to prove to her – she already knew how much progress I had made. We were in this together to a certain extent, so the pressure was right off. It would also give her an opportunity to scrutinise my course management and all those aspects of the game that can't be judged from a lesson.

It was a glorious round. We were relaxed, chatting about our daughters and all sorts of stuff quite unrelated to the game. As a result, I played some absolutely blinding golf. We soon realised that I was playing a very good round indeed and a slight tension began to mount. I could tell she was wary of commenting on it and we both tried to remain calm.

But while calm is her natural state, it is not mine, so as I stood on the fifteenth tee at three over par my ever-fertile imagination started to kick up a gear. If I could string together three birdies in the last four holes (tough but certainly possible), I'd have my par round and the whole thing would be over there and then. Of course, my brain didn't just stop there. Oh no. Rarely does it ever let me off so lightly. Suddenly I had visions of camera crews and the world's press gathering round to meet this new wonder kid. The guy with such natural talent that at thirty-seven years of age he had managed to drop thirty-two shots not in twelve months but in five. I was gonna be the new Ballesteros. Seve stood beside me and sighed. He put his head in his hands.

So did my imagination stop there? Oh, by crikey no. I started to visualise a life on the tour within a couple of years. Seve looked on and slowly shook his head in despair. My beautiful, stress-free and effortless round was about to be destroyed by my own daft pressurising and imagination. I was getting wildly ahead of myself, and the golfing gods felt that I was taking the whole thing a little too flippantly. I was not giving their beautiful game the respect it deserved. Clearly, I needed to be taught a little lesson. And what they delivered was two double bogeys in the last four holes.

I can see now that it was a good lesson. The golfing gods were right to pull me down a peg or two – I really needed it. If I'd come in level for those four holes and shot a 74, it would have created a big problem. I'd have eased right off, believing it would be child's play from there on in, and if there is one thing that you can be sure about with golf, it's that it's never easy.

I shot a 78 and I was delighted. Some golfers play for forty years and never shoot in the 70s and here I was shooting a 78 just a few short months after being unable to break 100. It was the milestone that I had always felt would be the toughest to achieve and all I needed to do now was take a stroke a month off this score and I'd be there.

The manner in which it was achieved is worth noting. I have a dreadful tendency to experiment on the course, but when I play with Debbie I can't do that because I just look like a fool. Therefore, every shot was judged properly, there were no macho shots with seven irons when it should have been a six, no Ballesteros-style bravura, and as a result I strung together an excellent score. There is a lesson here, and I wish I'd paid more attention to it at the time. It's a lesson I still need drummed into me every time I play.

Another aspect of playing with a scratch golfer or a professional is that you slowly adopt their tempo and style of play, and that means taking time over a shot and using a full pre-shot routine. When playing with a bunch of hackers out for a laugh, you generally (or I do anyway) adopt that style, too, but out with a pro, you get a huge lift from just copying the way they play.

Stuart Kennedy – the friend who had quizzed Sam Torrance at the Royal County Down – had been following my progress with interest and when I talked to him about getting my handicap, he volunteered to play with me and sign my final card. He was a nominal 16-handicapper who had in the past played at a much better level but who had been affected by the 'shanks' a few years previously and had basically given up the game.

So off we went for the third and final round of my handicap cards. I stood on the first tee and shot one of my usual booming drives down the fairway to expressions of awe from Stuart.

'That's incredible, John – I really didn't expect you to be

playing like that. I'm not going to blow smoke up your ass in an unjustified way, but that is amazing ball striking.'

'Cheers, Stuart, appreciate that. I don't always do that but it's probably the best part of my game,' I replied.

'Well, I tell you what. If you can strike a ball like that at this stage, then I don't think you'll have any problems.'

The conditions were very similar to the day I shot my 78 and I was feeling confident. If I could just hold it together, I might beat that score and boost my confidence even more. Once again, however, the fragility of my mental game let me down. I shot a 90. A twelve-shot swing in four days. I'd simply eased off my concentration in the light of Stuart's positive comments and lost some focus. I was trying to impress him off the tee and maybe got overly brave on some other shots. It's hard to put a finger on any one aspect of my game that let me down – simply put, my golf was worse at every level.

Without a shadow of a doubt, this clearly showed that I needed to pay more attention to how I dealt with the pressures of playing on the course with different people and in conditions that weren't one hundred per cent perfect. This is a crucial part of the game and it continued to be a major part of my challenge throughout the year.

I had enjoyed playing with Stuart, though, and he became my main playing partner during the rest of the challenge. His naturally competitive nature and excellent course-management skills kept me motivated and helped me get the game into perspective. I learned a lot from him during that winter.

So with all my cards marked, I handed them in to the handicap committee at the end of October. It was an odd sequence of cards – no doubt about it. A 78, a 90 and a 95. The committee looked at them in a puzzled way and fed the information into the computer. Out popped my handicap – 14. It was a reasonable measure of where I was and yet I was slightly annoyed that I hadn't managed to string together three decent rounds to get a better handicap. I felt it was a shame that I hadn't put in three cards at the very beginning of the challenge to show my progress more effectively, but that was not the way I'd wanted to proceed. It was never about handicaps. It was about the pursuit of one level-par round on my own terms and in my own way.

My way made sure that I didn't get embroiled in standard club issues and the competition process. I didn't have any spare time to devote to playing the various matches and would have found all the waiting around and socialising infuriating. It's not that I'm an unsociable person, it's just that club events take up a huge amount of time and, in my situation at least, would detract from the process of actually getting better at golf.

Having said that, when I was awarded my handicap certificate, I began to think about how quickly I could get down to scratch. I dithered about for a while and, spurred on by my progress, thought about setting myself a secondary challenge of getting a scratch handicap within the next year. This then became a distraction from my present, crystal-clear goal and a good friend advised me to keep my focus on the current challenge, and see what happened after that. Wise words, and for once I heeded them.

Taking Stock

Some men see things as they are and say, 'Why?'
I dream of things that never were and say,
'Why not?'

With autumn drawing to a close, I sat in the bar at Blackwood
one afternoon and looked out over the course. I was trying to
assess my game but the splendour of the surroundings struck me
once again. Originally the brainchild of the Marchioness of
Dufferin and Ava, who owns the land and the nearby Clandeboye
Estate, Lady Dufferin wanted to create not only a beautiful golf
course but one whose membership was not restricted to the usual
wealthier sections of society. Great golf for the masses, as it were.

The setting is spectacular – mature woodland boasting some
of the rarest trees in Ireland. A fabulous source for mushrooms
during autumn, for years I (and many others) had foraged about
in the woods, searching for porcini, often arriving home with
great armfuls that would have cost three fortunes in the fancy
restaurants of London. Blackwood Golf Centre also boasted the
incredible Michelin-starred Shanks restaurant run by the late
Robbie Millar, a true culinary genius, and his wife Shirley. The
course and its setting were very dear to my heart.

Sitting at the bar that day, I reflected on the marvellous journey I'd travelled so far and what a wonderful privilege it was to
be able to live out my fantasy at Blackwood. Taking stock of my

game as if it were a business venture, I tried to pinpoint my weaknesses to see more clearly what it was I needed to concentrate on. In business there are very few problems that can't be resolved with a bit of methodical and rational thinking and a decent, prioritised plan of action. This approach hadn't always been at the forefront of my mind with regard to the challenge, because golf was an emotional outlet for me. When I put my sensible business head on, however, it could be analysed and dealt with like any other business problem.

The clock was ticking, and ticking increasingly fast. There is no doubt that I'd made some great progress alongside some very fundamental mistakes. But those mistakes were necessary. I don't believe I could have made such progress if I'd simply stuck to the advice or programme set by any one individual. Nobody had achieved what I was attempting, so inevitably it would require a lot of new thought and a bit of bravery to try out new tactics. The key thing I had to bear in mind was to recognise when I was in a dead end and quickly get out of it and move forward again. I had benefited greatly from a combination of the solid and consistent advice of Debbie and the principles of Jim McLellan. This, coupled with a huge amount of practice, meant I'd created a very good swing and at some level an ability to score half decently as well.

My assessment at this stage looked like this:

PUTTING

I was relatively happy with my putting, although there was clearly a level of denial going on. I hated, and still do hate, putting practice and was labouring under the illusion that the putting green would be open all winter and I'd work away at it then. I was generally shooting thirty-six putts per round or less, so I didn't feel there was any major issue there.

DRIVING

My driving was the best part of my game. The main emphasis of my practice had been towards the development of a good full swing, and driving is the ultimate manifestation of this. In the right conditions, I was capable of regularly hitting 300-yard drives. Take off the inevitable macho nonsense and exaggeration inherent in that statement and you're still left with a good driving ability.

At approximately 6,300 yards, the Hamilton course at Blackwood is not a huge course and I could manage to turn eight of the par-four holes into a drive and a wedge, which greatly helped my scoring potential. Part of the premise of the challenge had been to focus my game closely on the Hamilton course and avoid learning shots that were redundant. Being able to drive and wedge so many holes totally transformed the level of work I needed to do on my game. It is also a relatively straight course, so there was no need to be able to draw or fade the ball at will. I looked on in envy at friends who could do this, but with only a year to create the sort of swing required to shoot a par round, I felt my priority had to be on keeping it simple and hitting the ball straight. Seve's earlier advice was correct and learning to fade or draw, although great for the ego, seemed to be a recipe for months of frustration and possibly ruining the progress I had made so far. It was a shot-making luxury that I couldn't, and didn't need to, afford. I was very happy with my TaylorMade driver, too, and this helped to increase my confidence.

FAIRWAY WOODS

I had high levels of confidence with my old Mizuno three wood and this had transferred well to the new Ping. Hitting a three wood was rare for me, though, such was my confidence with the driver, and it might only come out of the bag two or three times per round as a second shot on the par-five holes. This allowed me to narrow my choice of clubs to driver, three wood and wedge, effectively playing to my strengths again.

LONG IRONS

The cautious decision to opt for cavity-back 'game improvement' irons was definitely the right one and I had high levels of confidence in this area. Once more, though, the combination of my good driving and the set-up at Blackwood meant that I didn't need anything lower than a six iron, unless I messed up.

SHORT IRONS

My basic ball-striking ability with the short irons was good but this was a classic area where my game was affected by becoming too much of a range jockey. My ball-striking on less-than-perfect lies was often very poor and my ability to judge how many extra clubs to use in windy situations was very poor also. My experimentation with the different wedges on course was frequently having an adverse effect on my scoring. On countless occasions an arrow-straight 300-yard drive (take large pinch of special golfer's BS salt as necessary) would regularly be converted to a bogey simply by making foolish decisions on which wedge to use and not striking it cleanly. There was a small piece of ground at the side of the par-three course that I was planning to use to develop my ball-striking practice in more realistic grass-lie situations.

PITCHING/CHIPPING

My pitching and chipping were very variable. Again, progress here was curtailed by too much range work and not enough creative practice out on grass of variable quality. The lack of a public grass practice area at Blackwood meant that it was difficult to practise this part of my game properly without actually playing a round. But this was just an excuse really. I could have easily found grass to practise on and merely chose to use the comfort zone of the range and the covered bays.

My basic ball-striking was good as a result of having had to practise so much when my wrist was injured, but a tough lie and a hazard such as a bunker in front of me meant that my confidence would collapse and I would regularly fluff the shot. My ability to judge the run, using various clubs for chipping, was also poor. It all boiled down to a requirement to get out and play more or find some way to practise in more realistic conditions.

COURSE MANAGEMENT

Rubbish. Macho, I-can-be-Seve-in-1979 rubbish. Undoubtedly, I'd created a good swing and had some ball-striking ability but time and time again I would throw away what could otherwise have been good scores with silly mistakes and stupid club selection decisions. My fictional mentorship by Seve was great in many ways but it caused me a lot of problems when it moved past this phase and into I-can-do-that-too adulation. Seve had created so many amazing shots out of nowhere at the height of his career that this was hard-wired into me as something to aspire to.

The problem was, I didn't have an ounce of the raw talent and creativity that Seve had, and it's probably worth bearing in mind that Seve was the only golfer who had ever managed to be consistently successful with that style of play. Even he calmed things down enormously in the later years of his own professional career, but this type of logic would often elude my thinking when I was out on the course. I generally never took the safe option and was always trying to eke out a club rather than take another and hit it gently.

The classic example of this 'Seve' mentality was when I was faced with a tree in my path. I would always assume I could hit through it and would never dream of playing around it and making up the shot elsewhere. Practically every instructional manual by highly successful golfers advocates taking your punishment and chipping out, but naively, or perhaps arrogantly, I would presume that that didn't apply to me.

Stuart has excellent course-management skills and he helped me enormously at this point in the challenge. Every game with him involved a lesson in the harsh realities of playing skilfully and trying to score, rather than just striking the ball well. Once, when we were playing the tenth hole at Blackwood, I put my drive to the right of the fairway with a tree blocking my way. The obvious solution was to play a relatively safe shot to the left of the tree and try to rescue par with my short game. Needless to say, I blasted the ball through the trees and caught a branch. The ball landed a few yards further down the fairway.

It was a pivotal moment.

Stuart stopped and said: 'Hang on, hang on. Before we move on I want to ask you a question. Were you lucky with that shot or unlucky? Now, think about your answer.'

With not a second's thought, I immediately replied, 'Unlucky of course! I hit the tree. How could I be lucky to have hit the tree?'

'Well,' he replied, 'in my book you were lucky. You played a stupid shot and were lucky to get away with it. You could easily have ended up in the stream or even with the ball back in your face.'

I paused to let this sink in. 'Fair enough,' I said. 'I see what you mean. I never thought about it like that.'

'Well, John, you have got to start to think about golf like this and stop just bashing away as hard as you can,' he continued. 'You need to get out there and play with some excellent players and see what they do. Their game will be a million miles different from the way you play!'

'Yeah, I know. It's just difficult to organise the time to play and, to be honest, I don't know anybody who plays at that level.'

'Well, get out the videos then. Get onto eBay and buy a load of old tournament videos. Ignore all the bravado shots but concentrate on how the great guys get out of trouble and take their medicine. You'll be surprised at how many of them still save par, even after an appalling drive and a cautious safety shot. I can't emphasise this enough. Forget about the mechanics for a while and learn some course management.'

Whatever viewpoint you take, it was an eye-opening experience for me, and very, very slowly I began to look at the game from a slightly different perspective. The perspective of playing percentage golf and trying to save par without giving myself double and triple-bogey opportunities. It was a very slow process, though, and that day, within seven holes, I was again trying to hit the ball through a tree and forgetting Stuart's wise words of little more than an hour earlier. The fact that I got away with it this time probably did me no favours in the long term and I can still see Stuart walking down the fairway in front of me shaking his head in exasperation.

Another aspect of my course management that Stuart helped me with was the management of wind. On a windy day I was consistently under-clubbing and Stuart helped me to grasp the notion of whether a wind was one, two or three clubs in strength.

We'd stand at the tee box and he'd ask: 'OK, we've 165 yards
– what would you play normally?'

'Seven iron.'

'But the wind is blowing today. How many clubs is that
wind?'

'It's an extra club for sure. A firm six, I reckon.'

'John – that's a three-club wind. Look at how it affected us on
the last hole and look how it's blowing the trees up there. You
hit a six iron here today and it'll just be held in the air, static. It's
a four iron punched low.'

As ever, he was correct. Time and again touring professionals
are asked to comment on the major problem they observe in
amateurs' play in the Pro-Am tournaments. More than ninety
per cent of the time the answer is that they see amateurs under-
clubbing and not reaching the green. I was firmly in that
category. Always, always, *always* short and never long. Two
beautifully struck approach shots maybe, but left struggling for
par, just because I couldn't judge properly how far I needed to
hit the ball.

MENTAL GAME

It was clear that my mental game still needed a lot of work.
Winter was looming and although I could already break 80 and
I felt there was plenty of time to dig deep into the vast amount
that has been written on this subject in the coming months, I
couldn't afford to ignore this aspect of my game for long. There
is no doubt that the pressures of the challenge meant that my
requirement for a strong mental attitude was even more important than it is for most golfers. My handicap scores particularly
highlighted just how much I needed to concentrate on my
mental game. A swing of seventeen strokes between rounds in
similar conditions indicated much more about my mental state
than anything else.

I viewed every round from a different perspective to the
average golfer. It was ultimately an odd form of the game I
was developing – predominantly based around one course and
the shots that I would need to score there. It wasn't about

developing an ability to play links golf, or even how to deal with matchplay or competition situations. It was a slightly unusual and restrictive type of golf. That's what the challenge consisted of and there was no point in trying to develop my game outside of these boundaries. Playing regularly with Stuart, however, did help to shift my focus away from the ultimate goal and towards our own matchplay games. I'd a tendency to give up when I played a bad front nine, because my score was ruined. Our matches helped me retain a competitive focus throughout the full eighteen holes, which was very useful. Winter league golf would undoubtedly have helped with this, too, but I felt that it just wasn't right for me at that time.

FAMILY LIFE

I was continuing to hold this together pretty well. Aside from a few exasperated remarks from both Lesley and Aimee, spoken more in jest than anything else, my work on the challenge impacted very little on Aimee's life. I went to work as usual and came home as usual. I only went to the range after she had gone to bed, and weekend golf was generally confined to a Sunday morning and maybe a couple of hours on a Saturday afternoon when she was usually at some activity or at a friend's party. With Lesley, I had learnt my lesson from the sledgehammer incident and was trying my (possibly useless) best to keep my clutter to a minimum. I could tell she was occasionally disgruntled but, as ever, she never voiced her annoyance and managed to continue to be enormously supportive and encouraging, whether things were going well or badly. She even listened with endless patience to my latest breakthroughs and daft ideas which I believed would make it all so easy in the coming months.

WORK

I was also keeping work pretty much under control. It would be fair to say that my attention wasn't always one hundred per cent on the job, but my business partners continued to be very supportive even if they were inwardly exasperated at some of my absences. They must have frequently wondered just where it was exactly that I was having my 'lunch'.

By this stage I realised that the nature of the challenge had changed. What had started out ten years previously as an idle piece of chitchat had morphed into something that was really just about me and golf. The cyclist Lance Armstrong's inspirational book, *It's Not About the Bike*, relates his remarkable recovery from cancer and the journey back to his Tour de France win in 1999. When I was initially questioned about my challenge, I often borrowed his title, replying: 'It's not about the golf.' Yet now I believed that golf was what it was precisely about. I had become totally immersed in the game, not merely in the process of getting better.

In my mind's eye I could still see myself as I was over twenty years ago, fired up by Seve's magnificent win at the Irish Open in Dublin. Yet I had allowed myself to be dissuaded from the notion of becoming a professional. The challenge had partly become about me trying to prove to myself – and that fifteen-year-old boy – that I *could* do it. If I could shoot par in a challenge like this at the age of thirty-seven, then surely there would have been enough talent in that boy to have played at least journeyman pro level?

I didn't need, or even want, to go shouting 'I told you so' to anyone else, but I wanted to sit down in my mind with fifteen-year-old Johnnie and Seve and say, 'See, I knew I could do it. I knew deep down that I was capable of playing great golf.' I wanted to give that awkward teenager a bit of the adult confidence that we all lack at that age. Ultimately it wouldn't make any tangible difference, but it was important to me.

Back in May, my plan had been to generate maximum media interest in the challenge, as if it were just like any other commercial venture I was involved in. But now none of that seemed to matter so much. It even seemed at odds with the spirit of the thing. In my quiet times on the range, with the rain lashing in on me, it seemed that it was important for me to endure a certain amount of pain, just like all the greats had, before I could earn my right to any level of breakthrough. An old Jack Nicklaus video really brought it home to me. Sitting with his long-term coach, Jack Grout, talking about playing all winter long in Ohio, Nicklaus recalled how he had bashed every available ball out into the snow and had to wait to spring before they could collect them. The romance of that image appealed enormously to me.

I needed to pay my dues to the game and not shout too loudly about how great I thought I was and how easy my progress had been. I had been bitten too badly on the ass each time I got above myself and I was wary of too much self-promotion. And pay my dues I did. Standing at the range day after day, in the immortal words of Ben Hogan, I'd 'dig dirt'. Digging dirt with a silent audience of Hogan, Ballesteros, Jones, Palmer and Nicklaus all bashing away beside me in adjoining bays. All committed to a Zen-like state of pursuing excellence.

The Mental Game

Always bear in mind that your own resolution to
succeed is more important than any one thing.

ABRAHAM LINCOLN

For a while now I had been idly reading a few books on the
subject of the mental game but hadn't really focused too heavily
on any of them. Rotella had been hugely inspirational to me in
the early days, but more from a get-off-your-fat-ass perspective
than from a here-is-exactly-how-to-control-your-mind one.
Gallwey's *Inner Game of Golf* had impressed, too, but, ultimately,
I got the feeling that his heart wasn't really in golf. It seemed to
be more of a simple follow-up to his tennis books. Having said
that, I could see a lot of sense in his proposition that you need
to come up with some trigger during the swing to try to switch
the mind off.

I bought a CD course from Dr Karl Morris, who works closely
with many of the tour players, including Darren Clarke. Clarke
is something of a golfing god here in Northern Ireland, so that
was a strong motivator for me to try Morris out. Karl's course is
excellent and his advice on 'quieting' the mind during putting is
exceptional. I listened to it many times on the long journeys
between the two garden centres, and finally started to become
fascinated by the whole mental game.

In relation to putting, Morris talks extensively about the use
of the creative side of the brain (the right side). If you are looking

creatively at something, then it will show as activity on the right. A study showed that excellent putters use this side of their brain more than the left during putting. If you are trying to work through specific, logical actions, then this will show up as activity in the left side.

This right-side activity seemed to indicate that putting was more about using and trusting your creative instincts than it was about a perfect stroke and geometric analysis. This made a tremendous amount of sense to me. I've always felt that putting is a vastly over-complicated process and that's what makes so many people get the yips and freeze over the ball. The often-used analogy is that you can take your keys out of your pocket and throw them to somebody on the other side of the room with ninety-nine per cent accuracy most of the time. So why can't we hole putts in such an intuitive way? You certainly don't need to spend hours looking at the keys and nobody would ever consider taking a practice throw. Morris's observations emphatically backed up my own thinking on the matter and helped me approach putting from a different perspective.

With driving the strongest part of my game and putting the weakest, the following statistics from an issue of *Today's Golfer* magazine struck a chord with me:

- The top ten longest drivers on the European Tour averaged winnings of £12,958.
- The top ten putters (lowest putts per round) averaged £61,160.

I also found a wonderful statistical comparison between a bogey golfer (an 18-handicapper) and a scratch golfer taken from an old 1996 article in *Golf Magazine*. The scratch golfer drives, on average, only 17 yards longer than the bogey golfer, and he hits the fairway only twice more per round. The difference lies in the fact that of the seven shots that Bogey misses, the five that land on the fairway cannot be advanced normally – that is, they are obstructed in some way. Only one of Scratch's five cannot be advanced normally. The article proposed that one reason bogey players miss the fairway so wildly is that they strive to be long from the tee – which sounded, and still sounds, all too familiar to me.

Scratch then proceeds to hit seventy-two per cent of greens when approaching from the fairway and fifty-five per cent from the rough, which is about double Bogey's percentages. This translates into twelve out of eighteen greens hit in regulation by Scratch, while Bogey hits only four. This is where my golf was falling down, too. I was driving like a scratch player but my approaches were firmly in the bogey camp. Poor club selection and woeful course management meant that I was regularly wasting all the advantage my huge booming drives were giving me. I didn't keep statistics but I didn't need to – it was as clear as a punch in the face when I read this.

But the really big difference was found in the short game. Scratch is three times more likely to hit the ball to within 5 feet of the hole from 50 yards (forty-seven per cent versus sixteen per cent) and Bogey is five times as likely to miss the green completely (four per cent versus sixteen per cent). While Scratch may miss six greens per round, he balances this by averaging six one-putts per round. Scratchy's average of thirty putts per round is four less than the Bogey man's, despite having similar first putt lengths of 15 and 17 feet respectively.

These statistics highlight what I, and I suspect most golfers, already know – that the big gains in our golfing ability come from the short game and not our driving ability. We all know this but we still choose to ignore it. The Holy Grail for most of us continues to be the ability to hit huge drives to impress our friends.

A conversation with Jason Carlton, a highly successful marketing copywriter, who had been responsible for the sale of a large variety of golf instructional manuals over many years, confirmed this claim. Publishers had reached a stage, he said, where they simply didn't bother promoting short game or putting-instruction manuals because they didn't sell. At best they are bundled as freebies along with the latest add-40-yards-instantly-to-your-drives package. Instant gratification is what we all desire and that has got to be the major factor in the huge growth and development of the driver industry. It promises to deliver those extra yards we all crave, without having to take a single lesson or hit a single ball in practice. A good illustration of this point is that no one notices Tiger's astonishing ability to rattle long putts under pressure – all they rave about are his 350-yard drives and how the classic old courses of the world have to be lengthened to 'tame the Tiger'.

Time and time again, I fell into this trap myself. My putting practice overall totalled no more than five hours, and although I had spent a decent amount of time on my pitching and chipping, it was completely dwarfed by the number of hours I'd spent bashing away with my driver and working on my full swing.

Nevertheless, in an odd sort of way, it was working. As October drew to an end, I played two exceptional rounds of golf. Stuart and I played regularly in the evenings and had developed an excellent rhythm. I enjoyed our games, and my knowledge and understanding of how best to play Blackwood was improving greatly, too.

Reading so much about the mental game had also improved my practice routine, and it now had much greater focus. I was frequently mentally rehearsing the course in the evenings at home and I would play the entire course in my head from the comfort of the range, visualising every shot in relation to each hole. I would start by hitting a driver and full pitching wedge for the first hole, proceed to driver, three wood and pitch over the bunker to the par-five second hole, and continue like this until I had played the whole course. I would find that on the range I was maybe only hitting two or three bad shots throughout this imaginary round, which, in turn, was starting to translate into some much more encouraging scoring on the course.

This process was just one part of a tightly developed routine for my practice. Gradually, I started hitting fewer balls but with much better results. Not only did this help me to avoid the wrist and elbow injuries I had suffered in the first couple of months, but it meant that practice became more fun. If I wanted to work on one aspect of my game, I'd simply use one of the various techniques I'd developed for that and work away until I got bored. I'd then use another technique to continue that part of my practice or switch to something else. This added variety to my practice sessions. It was no longer a case of endlessly bashing drives and, when I got tired of that, trying to see if I could hit the back fence. I was now concentrating on the specific parts of my game that required work, without regarding it as a chore.

I still had six full months to go, and playing in autumn on the beautiful parkland course was a joy. Out with Stuart, I managed once to play fifteen holes in four over par, and a more memorable sixteen holes in two over. On both occasions we ran out of light but the latter round, in particular, showed just how high my levels of confidence were at this stage and how well my golf was flowing. It seemed like the end result would be just a matter of weeks away. As I stood on the seventeenth tee in near pitch-darkness I was desperate to play the last two holes to see if I could birdie them. But it was cold as well as dark, and Stuart persuaded me to call it a day and head home.

If I'd been putting at all well at that stage, I'd most likely have been under par. I still believed that all my putting woes would be sorted in the winter and that by spring all would be well. As long as I could keep up the rest of my momentum, then the par round would be easy. If only I'd bothered to look across at Seve in my passenger seat when I got into the car, I'd have seen him muttering 'dick' under his breath and shaking his head in exasperation. Yet again.

It was around this time that Stuart managed to blag himself the invitation to the Jaguar corporate day at the Royal County Down. An invitation not just to mix with the great and the good who might buy one of those fabulous cars, but also to meet the legendary Sam Torrance. The hero of eight Ryder Cups and the man who sank the winning putt in 1985 that finally ended the American twenty-eight-year winning streak, Sam was well known for being a straight talker. And it was at this event that he delivered his 'dream on' verdict when Stuart asked about my chances of success. Two words that would come to haunt and motivate me in equal measure over the next months. Two words that would ultimately encapsulate what the whole challenge meant for me. Two words that changed my life.

Rather than shake my confidence, at that stage Sam's remark was the perfect motivator. It strengthened my will to succeed and made me double my efforts. But way off in the distance, though at that time invisible to me, a tiny speck was appearing; the clouds of doubt were starting to gather. Soon they would roll across the wintry skies of Ulster.

Winter Closes In

All our dreams can come true, if we have the
courage to pursue them.

WALT DISNEY

Then, once again, I managed to injure myself and restrict my practice. This time it wasn't through too much golf but happened
when I was swimming with my daughter. I didn't want to be an
absent father during the challenge and spent a fair amount of time
overcompensating with Aimee. My paternal discipline (lax at the
best of times) was even more relaxed than usual and I would tend
to buy her more treats than normal. When we were together I
would make very sure that I was one hundred per cent engaged
with her and not sitting reading a newspaper or nodding in absent-
minded agreement as she chatted. Likewise, going swimming did
not involve me drifting lazily around the pool while she splashed
about. It was an endless round of dolphin rides, standing on my
hands and generally behaving like a fool to entertain her. I could
then nip up to the range afterwards with a relatively guilt-free
conscience. The Irish term for the way I behaved in the pool was
'acting the eejit' and, as a result, I pulled a muscle in my elbow.

The injury effectively meant no full swinging for a few weeks.
In the meantime, I chose, as ever, not to concentrate on my
putting but to work on my chipping. (Heaven forbid I would
use the time productively with a putter.)

When I'd had any injuries in the past, I had chosen to work

on my pitching and lob-wedge shots since obviously these are the 'glamour' part of the short game. Lob it up or pitch with some spin and the crowds ooh and ah in your imagination. Chipping practice is a fraction too close to putting practice for my liking and, as a result, had managed to be relegated to the 'if I've any time left' section of any session. Not surprisingly I never did have any time left.

So, to try to develop my skills in this area, I used the age-old practice of creating a little personal competition to spur myself on. I had hit a few dozen pitches to a distance of 20 feet or so. One of the balls, I noticed, was a different colour to the rest and I decided to chip until I hit that ball. Then, and only then would I allow myself to go home. I guessed that it would take about thirty or forty shots.

By the time I had hit a hundred chips without managing contact, I was, to say the very least, more than a little put out. By the time I had hit 150, I was almost crying with frustration. The Zen-like joy of practice went out the window. I was like a man possessed, and nothing could have dragged me home before I made contact. The range was empty by now and my pile of balls sprayed out like a comet's tail from the one I'd been trying to hit. At 180 chips and with the range closing in five minutes, I finally hit the damn thing.

I felt shaken by the experience, and with great trepidation I tried the same drill a few days later. This time I managed it in forty-seven shots. My worst score wasn't 180, though – on one occasion it took me over two hundred chips to connect with the ball. This drill certainly never became the mainstay of my practice routine, but I used it now and again to punish myself for neglecting my short game and to fire up the competitive streak to improve my score.

By the middle of November I realised that my arm injury was more serious than I first thought. Although my chipping had benefited, it meant that I still couldn't play any rounds. On top of this, the weather became as revolting as only Northern Ireland winter weather can be and the course had moved to temporary greens.

I had no option but to ease off for a while, which, in the short term, did me no harm at all. Life had been hectic for long enough and my view is that these things naturally ebb and flow and you can't be running at a hundred miles an hour all the time. My confidence was high, possibly too high for my own good, but I was concerned about my fitness levels. I seemed to be falling prey to injuries rather too frequently and having setbacks as a result. I was worried that I'd reach the last few months when I'd need to be playing several times a week and I'd have an injury that would prevent me from doing so.

My home set-up of weighted club, legendary sledgehammer and elastic exercise band didn't seem to be doing the job, so I joined a gym. With the help of an instructor, I worked out a routine to increase my general strength, fitness and flexibility. We worked on very little that wouldn't be of specific benefit to me on the course and with my swing. I needed all the muscles that I used when swinging to be as strong and flexible as possible.

The problem was that this started to become an end in itself. My golf obsession was slightly sidetracked and for a brief while I teetered on the brink of a fitness obsession. It always seemed a lot easier to go to the gym than brave the course. After all, hadn't I been bagging excellent scores in the autumn and wasn't the weather just as foul as it could be? There is no doubt that getting fit was an important part of the process but it was gaining precedence over my game. Time that I would have previously allocated for the range at lunch hour was now earmarked for the gym and my increasingly misguided quest for ultra-fitness.

My full routine took the best part of an hour. Travel and shower time meant that I would be away from work or family for nearly two hours. When I was visiting the gym three of four times a week that meant six to eight hours away from improving my golf.

Undoubtedly I did get a lot fitter, but after my injury had healed, I'd have become eighty per cent as fit by taking this time to run round the par-three course with a heavy bag three times a week and continuing to work with my sledgehammer, elastic band and weighted club at home while watching a golf video or TV.

It just goes to show how easily you can become distracted during any sort of challenge. With the very limited time available to me, this fitness kick was almost certainly a mistake. It was actually just the 'easy' option and part of my challenge fantasy. I had always imagined a bit of gym time in my movie montage and this was just me foolishly living out that dream. And as I acted out my *Rocky* fantasy, Seve would sit quietly on the bench beside me with his head in his hands.

My original plan to use the winter months to practise my putting was well and truly scuppered. In casual conversation with Debbie about my putting progress, she informed me that the putting green was closed from November to the start of April. This was a proper 'Oh shit' moment, but I have to admit that I didn't actively look for other solutions. A secret part of me was actually punching the air, rejoicing in the fact that I now had a legitimate excuse not to practise my putting.

'Dick,' I heard Seve mutter.

And then Christmas arrived. It was tough for a variety of reasons. Garden centres are as busy during the festive season, selling decorations and gifts, as they are during the spring and summer, selling plants and outdoor furniture. I had been royally chancing my arm with my fellow directors during the previous few months and I needed to knuckle down now and do some hard work to ensure that Christmas was a commercial success.

The combination of this extra work, the bad weather and my injury meant that I hadn't been able to play much, which was starting to cause me some concern. My confidence began to evaporate at a frightening speed and privately I was beginning to get a little worn down by the process. Of greater concern was that I knew I would see lots of friends and family members over the Christmas period, many of whom were good, experienced golfers. With my confidence plummeting, I wasn't looking forward to the sheer volume of 'no chance, mate' comments I knew were coming my way. It's easy to be strong in the face of people saying 'It can't be done' if they're keyboard warriors on the other side of the world. But when it's someone you know and respect who's telling you calmly to your face that it can't be done, well, that's an entirely different matter. And when they use guarded, doubting expressions and talk in a measured and plausible way about the difficulties you will face, but then wish you luck, the effect can be catastrophic. They may not mean to scupper your chances, but their words and body language can really shatter an already fragile confidence. Confidence, unless you are a Tiger Woods or a Donald Trump, is a fragile thing.

Tiger's confidence is, of course, not the basis of any normal development situation. He has, through the efforts of his late father, developed a huge level of self-belief over the years. One of the many Tiger stories that sticks with me is the one about his practice regime as a teenager. His father would stand beside him and hurl abuse to try and distract him as he played. This was based on experience that he had developed as a soldier in Vietnam and it goes some way to explain how Tiger can be so resilient out on the course. All that talk about Tiger not being mortal and his talent being otherworldly is utter rubbish. He has just worked much harder and much more effectively with the natural talent that he has than any other golfer.

I, of course, did not have a father who went to Vietnam to learn how to hurl abuse at me in my teenage years – certainly not for my golfing ability, anyway. As a result of standard unpleasant teenage-boy behaviour perhaps, but not to improve my golf. As a consequence, my resilience is not Tiger-like and many of these 'it can't be done' conversations had a strong effect upon me.

One conversation in particular was very annoying. At a large party I ended up talking to a pompous old buffoon who had heard about my challenge. He talked to me in a patronisingly dismissive way about my progress so far, no matter how polite and pleasant I tried to remain.

'You do understand that just because you shot a couple of rounds in the 70s there is no way that you'll get to par before May?' he said.

'Well, I'm not sure I agree.' I was already bristling at the loaded question but stayed outwardly calm. 'I accept that it's harder but I've already taken thirty-odd shots off my game so far.'

'Yes, but the last few shots are a nightmare to shed. Trust me, I've been playing this game for forty years and there's nothing you can tell me about it. What is your handicap now?'

This was going in the wrong direction.

'Well, it's 14 but – '

'And you want to get to scratch in five months? No chance,' he interrupted.

'No – I want to play one level-par round in five months.'

'Well, it's still not possible,' he said again. 'It can take years to lose those last few shots. Years. What makes you think you know better than all those golfers playing every day around the world?'

'I'm not saying I know better.' It was becoming impossible to hide my annoyance. 'I've just set myself a challenge and I've made huge progress so far. I see no reason why I can't do it.'

'Five winter months and your very best round after a summer of solid play was 78? No chance.'

Every sentence was delivered with a dismissive smirk and patronising tone of voice. If I hadn't been a polite, wee, middle-class fella, I'd have told him to sod off and just walked away. As it was, I felt trapped and claustrophobic. I'd had far too many of these conversations recently and they were wearing me down.

Another conversation, although outwardly more supportive, yielded an odd statement that has stuck with me and, I think, says a tremendous amount about golfers and their mental comfort zones. This golfer remarked that his handicap had been as low as 4 but now he wasn't capable of being a 6-handicapper, even recently moving back to 10. I found this an utterly bizarre thing to say. No doubt there will be plenty of golfers who will nod sagely and agree with this in principle, but it makes no rational sense. It's so clearly rooted in self-image and comfort zones rather than any lack of golfing ability.

The way I've approached golf is very different from the vast majority of other golfers. I've exposed myself to practically no nineteenth-hole-style chat and played with very few people who had been at it a long time. I also pretty much refused to play with any folk who were sceptical of what I was trying to do. I felt pressured by their demands to see the extent of my progress.

As a result, I retained my naive, wide-eyed approach to golf, full of a teenager's sense of wonder and a belief in the possibility of all things. My heroes have always been those people who insist on doing things their own way, in face of all opposition, with flamboyance and perhaps an element of 'screw you'. Muhammad Ali, Ayrton Senna, Keith Richards and Seve Ballesteros were the type of people I looked up to. All very talented certainly, but also totally devoted to their craft and without an ounce of concern for what people thought of them.

This can-do approach of mine had lain dormant for over twenty years but now it had resurfaced as strong as ever, and was crucial to the success of my challenge. But very few club golfers think this way. Depending upon their generation, they may be inspired by Arnold Palmer, Seve Ballesteros or Tiger Woods, but when they take up the game themselves, their ambition is quickly shot down by the views of the low and mid-handicappers of their golf club.

Much of this stems from the fact that the average handicap has remained at 17 for the past forty years, with the result that the views of, say, a 12-handicapper can be understandably taken as gospel by a beginner. These 12-handicappers are likely to be the best golfers with whom a beginner gets to play, because golfers play in packs of handicaps. Bombarded with tales about how tough the game is and how long it takes to get to a decent handicap, it won't take long before his attitude is influenced by the dominant mindset of golfers who play at this level. In other words, the average golfer is taught to lower his sights. And when that happens, he can kiss goodbye to any ardent desire he once had to try to be a Seve or a Tiger.

If you can avoid this pitfall and learn the way I and a few others have learned, it will be of enormous benefit to you. I talked this over with Mark McMurray, who was the original inspiration for the challenge, at this time and he agreed that such negative influence should be avoided at all costs. He started to play golf in his thirties with nothing more than a strong sense of his own ability to play sport at a very high level. His simple but hugely difficult aspiration was to shoot a 67 at Blackwood. Needless to say, such a goal incited ridicule and amusement in much the same way that my challenge did and he attracted the same sarcastic comments about the length of time he spent at the range during the winter months.

His attitude to golf was based not on it being a social activity but a sport that he wanted to excel at. His experience in basketball at an international level had taught him that if he played badly, the best thing he could do was to practise straight after the match. He simply transferred this attitude to golf. After playing a round, he would go into the clubhouse for one social lemonade and then get back out to the range to practise. When he finally shot his 67, it was dismissed by many as a result of his 'natural' sporting ability – certainly nothing to do with his self-belief and hard work. When you look at his accomplishment rationally, however, or view it from a non-golfer's perspective, it seems the most logical thing in the world. You work very hard at the sport and you get very good. Simple.

Like Mark, I see golf in a different way from many other golfers. If you believe you aren't a 6-handicapper then you won't be one – it's a self-fulfilling prophecy. Indeed, many of my problems during the next few months of the challenge were directly due to a lack of self-belief and a slow ebbing away of my confidence. Quite simply, I listened to too many negative comments over Christmas and started to think like an ordinary golfer. I stopped taking advice from Seve and Hogan and started valuing the dull opinions of club members. Big mistake.

Breakthrough Number Two

There is nothing like a dream to create the future.
Utopia today, flesh and blood tomorrow.

VICTOR HUGO

In January, with my elbow finally healed, I was visiting the range again as much as possible in the evenings but concentrating entirely on the mental side of the game in my reading. I was starting to look for answers beyond the world of traditional golf publications. I'd been reading a number of books about peak performance for business and sales professionals using a process called neuro-linguistic programming (NLP). My initial breakthrough in terms of modelling swings was actually an NLP process, but I didn't realise it then.

I stumbled across a technique, which Karl Morris also refers to, called 'anchoring'. You create a psychological anchor to a good feeling or a successful moment that you can draw on in the future. The process is relatively simple. A good analogy is the way that certain smells evoke strong memories from childhood. For example, when I smell a gorse bush, it takes me back instantly to a family picnic we once had with my grandfather. He died a great many years ago – before my ninth birthday, in fact – so I was quite young, but the image that is evoked and the sensation of sitting on the grass with my family around me is very clear. A happy moment, triggered purely by the smell of gorse.

In business, a salesman can anchor a moment in which he has

successfully completed a sale and use that to help him to make a cold call or lift his mood at some future time when he isn't feeling very confident. This anchor will help him to trigger those same feelings of power and being in control. Rather than fretting over a prospective sale and worrying about rejection, he uses the anchor to conjure up feelings of success and confidence.

It's a straightforward process and you can easily experiment with it. Play a piece of music that you really love and when you are feeling fantastic and singing along like a demented fool firmly press or stroke a part of your body. Your ear lobe or the back of your hand works well but it doesn't really matter where you anchor as long as it is a clearly defined area that is easy to remember. Every time in the future you have a great success or feel fantastic then do the same thing. This anchors the emotion to that touch. Later on, when you aren't feeling so good or need a lift of confidence, you simply repeat the pinch or stroke and the feeling will come back. The more you do it the better it works but it will work from the very first attempt.

I didn't fully grasp the concept until, almost by accident, I stumbled across it at the range one night. The great thing about all my range practice during the winter was that I generally had the place to myself (all except my trusty friend, Seve, of course). All the summer range jockeys had cleared off, and with a strong sense of self-righteousness, I'd stand at the chilly range, bashing away on my own. As long as I practised at a reasonable pace, I would keep warm. I'd even bought a couple of thermal vests to keep me cosy.

On this particular night everything was flowing brilliantly. All golfers, once they get past the complete hacker phase, have these moments when it just seems to come together. Well, I was having one of those nights. It was late and I was belting the most enormous drives, straight as an arrow, down to the back fence. All male golfers dream of hitting the back fence of their driving range – for many of us it's nearly as important as getting a good score, and for a few it's even more important. It implies virility and true power.

The Blackwood range legends revolve around the time that

Darren Clarke visited the course. He sent ball after ball not just over the fence but right onto the fairway on one of the par-three holes behind the fence. If I'd been looking to take on a challenge for commercial gain, I would have concentrated on driving at the range. The ideal product to market to male golfers is 'From hacker to one hundred balls over the back fence: the secrets to creating awe in the clubhouse.'

Normally you have a kind of breaking point with your swing when you're hitting it well. A point where it starts to fall apart if you try to hit it too hard. So I really started to belt the thing, but instead of reaching this breaking point, the ball just went further and further. Ball after ball into the fence. Even Seve was delighted. 'Now you've got eet, my friend!' he shouted. 'See wha' hard work can do? No more trying to take the easy way out!' I had truly made it. I had reached golfing nirvana. Because I was standing on my own and was astonished that I was hitting the ball so well, with every hit, I muttered 'incredible', 'unbelievable' as each shot, straight as an arrow, flew further than the last.

The feeling I had was something approaching euphoria, and each time I uttered 'incredible' I realised that I was probably anchoring that word to the feeling of being an invincible golfer. This was what Seve must have felt like at the Open Championship in 1984. I needed some way to bottle that feeling and the anchoring process would do that job perfectly.

I decided to add a further anchor to the feeling. I'd read about how Tiger anchors a good shot by spinning his club, and I reckoned that something like that might work for me. So my routine involved watching the perfectly hit drive disappear into the distance while I uttered the word 'incredible', and I'd smile and spin, or 'twizzle', the grip in my hand as I let the head of the club trace the path of the falling ball. Now I had two (or three, if you count the smile) anchors to use to pull back this feeling of invincibility.

I wouldn't use the process on anything other than an absolutely perfect shot. I needed to be anchored to that euphoric, Master of the Universe feeling and not just the simple pleasure of having hit a good shot. I wanted to be able to conjure up the feeling that I was standing there in my supergolfer outfit, with my Y-fronts on outside the suit, ready to take on the world.

The trick now was to make this work for me when I was playing a round. I needed to incorporate it into my pre-shot routine, so that I could somehow draw on that feeling when I was out on the course. If I could replace the nervous moments before I hit a shot with this feeling of euphoric invincibility, then surely it would benefit my golf. Theoretically at least, it would provide a link between range and course, which is always difficult to achieve.

I worked that night on perfecting a pre-shot routine that would incorporate this new angle. I'd stand behind the ball and cross an imaginary line, my 'commit' line. Then I'd start to visualise the perfect shot and flight path. I'd imagine every aspect of the ball flight and hear the sound as it landed. All the while, I'd be twizzling the grip, letting the club trace the imaginary path of the ball, and muttering the word 'incredible' to myself. Strangely, forcing myself to smile was just as important as the other two elements, because it helped to reinforce the feeling of joy and euphoria. I'd combine these verbal and physical anchors with the continuous visualisation of the shot until I reached a stage where it felt just right. Then I'd pull the trigger and go. It remained a very fluid process. No standing and staring over the ball and freezing, just a lot of waggling and keeping flexible until I'd start.

The next day at the range I worked on this routine again before every shot, even in practice. As is always the way with golf, my almost Ballesteros-like abilities of the previous night had deserted me a little, but I was still striking well and there was no doubt that my anchors were working. I found I could easily conjure up that feeling of invincibility and my usual doubts were replaced with a strong sense of 'I can really play this game well'. The process seemed to make sense; it tied in with a variety of books I'd been reading, as well as some of the specific golf-psychology literature, so the theory was fine, and within the confines of the range it certainly worked. The real test would be out on the course. So out I toddled to try to prove it.

First-tee nerves were rarely my problem. Partly because the first tee at Blackwood is not visible from the clubhouse, and partly because I seldom played in an environment where there was an audience. So my first shot on the course was as good as it normally was, but later in the round I definitely noticed an improvement. Like all golfers, various points around the course held anxieties for me – the third hole at Blackwood, for instance. This long and tricky par-three hole had instilled in me a strong feeling of apprehension. I always regarded it as more of a par four. But using my anchoring technique, I was able to stand up to the ball comfortably and let the feelings of invincibility wash over me. Likewise, at the ninth tee I unleashed the best drive I have ever struck at that hole just by triggering the anchor.

There were other holes that I'd played badly in the past and various other features that had caused me problems. It's very tough, for example, to keep a water feature out of your mind if you've sent your last three shots into it. Even in these situations, my new routine and the anchoring process made me feel much more optimistic when I was hitting the ball. Putting, as ever, let me down, but I still shot a nice, steady 80 and ended the day very happy with how the process had helped me. It still needed tweaking and a bit more work to make it instinctive, but there is no doubt that, for me, it was a breakthrough in mind control.

Fundamentals, Fundamentals, Fundamentals

> The key to realizing a dream is to focus not on success but significance – and then even the small steps and little victories along your path will take on greater meaning.
>
> OPRAH WINFREY

The Christmas period had been very difficult – no doubt about it. But with this latest breakthrough and the decent score out on the course, by mid-January it seemed like I'd banished the tough times again. It was, to quote the sublime Nina Simone, a new dawn, a new day and I was feeling good.

Of course it wasn't all plain sailing. The whole golf-is-ninety-per-cent-mental argument is a pile of nonsense generally spouted by folk who have spent many years perfecting their swing and then find that they are collapsing on the course. Yes, the control of your mental state is vital, but you still have to get the basics right and obtain a decent swing with good fundamentals or you're not going anywhere. In terms of the overall game, I'd say that it's fifty-fifty – fifty per cent physical ability and fifty per cent mental state.

I felt happy that I had now managed a decent breakthrough in my mental game but there still needed to be constant work on my physical swing. I rarely had full lessons with Debbie at this stage but we decided to devote a half-hour to looking closely at the fundamentals once more. Generally, I felt I was striking very well and believed my efforts needed to go towards my short game. Debbie, however, still wanted to make sure that I had no issues that might cause problems as we went into the last few months.

With a certain amount of cockiness, I bashed a few balls up the fairway, certain that she would be delighted. I expected her to 'ooh' at how well I was hitting the ball and tell me how wonderful I was and that my goal was bound to be reached in the next couple of weeks.

Except, of course, this didn't happen. Instead, and for the only time during the year, she actually got angry with me. Debbie doesn't do gratuitous praise. Well, maybe for the legions of kids she teaches every summer, but not for me. As I stood back after hitting a few balls, waiting for my praise, I was met with what can only be described as a cross face.

'John. I really didn't expect to be having to teach you the grip at this stage in the year,' she started, clearly exasperated.

'Eh? But look, I've been hitting it well.'

'Maybe, but you need to grasp this once and for all. We need to get these basics one hundred per cent correct if you're to have a chance of doing this thing. You're hitting it OK but I can already tell that you're compensating with your swing.'

'OK,' I replied sheepishly.

'You must get this right and keep it right. I can't believe that after eight months we're still at the grip.'

I could feel the twin spectres of Hogan and Seve standing beside her, scratching their chins and nodding their agreement as she spoke the words. My copy of Hogan's *Five Lessons* had lain dormant beside my bed for many months and I'd long since removed the image of his grip from my computer desktop. While I'd been trawling my way through all manner of daft mental-golf guff, looking for easy options to help me get better, my grip was slipping slowly back round to where it had been when I started. Fundamentals, Johnnie Boy, fundamentals. Fundamentals, fundamentals, and one more time – fundamentals.

The sticking to fundamentals is one of those lessons that I

learned the hard way in my working life. It reminded me of my sandwich business, which had expanded at a ferocious rate. We were growing too fast, and although the business was basically profitable, we had totally run out of cash. One of my business partners also acted as the accountant and, unknown to me and our other partner, had accrued huge personal debts.

One day we arrived at work to discover he had gone bankrupt and there were several huge holes in our accounts. Since it was a partnership, all our bank financing stopped on that day and the wonderful growing business very quickly turned into a nightmare. After the bankrupt partner left, we ran around like headless chickens pulling in cash from whatever source we could find to prop up the business and pay our suppliers, so that we could keep trading while we tried to refinance.

A large customer put us in touch with a man in his seventies who had previously helped him in a similar situation. This character was worth well in excess of £40 million and certainly had the financial wherewithal to rescue us. He arrived at the door in his gleaming Mercedes S500 but didn't cut much of a physical presence himself. He was small, wore a cheap brown suit and chain-smoked throughout the meeting.

'OK, boys – how much money did you make last week? Let's see where we are,' he asked.

'Well,' I spluttered, 'we don't know that. We haven't got our accounts for last year yet. How can we work out our profit for a week? There are four shops and a factory.'

'What do you mean, you can't work out your profit for a week?' he asked with a curious look. 'I have a big café in Bangor and this is what I do ...'

He took an old brown envelope from his pocket and, with the cigarette hanging from his mouth, started to write with a chewed Bic biro.

'At the start of the week I count all the stock in the shop. Everything. Every single thing. Every teabag, every sugar cube and every single item of food. And then do you know what I do?'

I glanced in a bemused fashion at my partner. 'Er ... no.'

'I record what I buy every day and record my sales every day.

At the end of the week I count up all the wages I have to pay and recount the stock. So what do you think I have then?'

Like a naive fool, with my fancy business-studies degree, I answered, 'Er ... mmm ... ehhh ...'

'I have my profit. I just take off the rent and a few other things and I have my profit. Every week. Every single week. I count at the start, count at the end, and record during the week. Now is that hard?'

'No, well, I suppose not. But what about depreciation and accruals?' I asked, trying to pretend that I grasped the whole thing and was at least as clever as he was.

He fixed me with a steely look. 'Forget 'em. They don't matter for this. I can include them afterwards. These are your fundamentals. These businesses are simple but you gotta know your fundamentals. This is how it works. You pay X for your food, Y for your wages and what's left is your profit contribution. Do that, and we'll know where you are. Now, will you do that for me?'

'OK,' I mumbled.

But I knew we wouldn't and I think he knew we wouldn't, too. We could never do that over all our shops and the factory. It would take up too much time and, anyway, you couldn't really tell how much money a business of our size was making with that method. Or so I thought.

So up he got, handed me the brown envelope covered with his spidery writing and jumped into his Mercedes. One week later he returned and asked for the figures. We mumbled and stuttered and made our excuses about being too busy trying to save the business. He fixed us with a cold stare, wished us good luck and left. I never saw him again.

Two weeks later we shut the doors on the business. We were unable to meet the demands of our creditors and had to lay off all thirty staff who worked in the factory. We sold the shops for a fraction of their true value and got together just enough money to stop us from going bankrupt. A harsh lesson. Particularly so, because we subsequently discovered that in the weeks before we sold the factory we had been making about £8,000 profit a week. We could easily have saved the business with a relatively small cash injection, and our friend with his sound fundamentals could have provided the money at the drop of a hat. Needless to say, in my next business and every business I've operated since then, the fundamentals are never ignored and we *always* calculate a weekly profit and loss.

Like the business model, if you don't get the fundamentals of a golf swing right, you're sunk. It's common sense and it certainly doesn't need a rocket scientist to work it out. A golfer with a great swing but no control of the mental game will still be able to strike the thing and get round the course with some ability to score. But take a golfer with great mental attitude and no swing, and he will take an awful lot of strokes to bash his way round.

Lesson number one, eight months previously, had been predominantly about grip, ball position and checking the angle of my feet, but twenty-five thousand balls hit in practice later and all three were out of alignment. Once again the ball and feet position were easy to fix but the grip required more work. It wasn't as bad as it was at the beginning but it did need a fair bit of determined effort to ensure it stayed correct this time.

It was a valuable lesson. A lesson from Debbie that was pure Ben Hogan. Keep it relatively simple and stick at the fundamentals. So I went home that night to read, for the third time, Hogan's *Five Lessons*, and soon I was back on track.

The 'Harrington' Moment

> Dreams come true. Without that possibility, nature
> would not incite us to have them.
>
> JOHN UPDIKE

At the end of January I contacted the golf magazines again to
tell them about my progress. I wrote to all the major UK month-
lies and *Golf Digest Ireland*. I wavered between hoping they
would all say 'How wonderful. You sound like a great fella –
let's come and have a look' and ignoring me altogether. I didn't
need any more distractions or pressure but at this stage I felt that
it would be a useful extra motivator if my challenge became
more widely acknowledged. At the very least, I wanted something to be on their desks, so that *when* (in true American fist-
pumping fashion I wasn't allowing an *if*) I achieved the
challenge, it didn't come out of the blue.

I didn't hear back from any of the UK magazines but got a call
from John Shortt of *Golf Digest Ireland*. John is a great guy and
soon put me at my ease. I had no compulsion to 'big myself up'
and felt comfortable enough to tell him about a few of the frustrations I'd encountered. He wanted to do a small piece intro-
ducing me and my challenge to his readers, and if they liked it,
the magazine would run a monthly progress report that I would
write. It would help my motivation without being too time-
consuming.

I continued to keep working on my pre-shot routine to create a naturally flowing process that would help me trigger off a great shot without getting too bogged down in all my swing thoughts. There is an old expression, 'Success leaves clues'. It's often used in sales to motivate new or struggling reps, who are encouraged to watch closely how the successful guys in the firm operate. But it applies equally well to golf, particularly in the use of a solid pre-shot routine.

If you watch ten high handicappers tee off and then ten very low handicappers, you'll find an astonishing difference. The high handicappers will almost certainly have a very basic, loose pre-shot routine, which will vary throughout the round. They will focus more at the beginning and lose concentration towards the end of the round. They will tend to do a lot more bashing at the ball with little thought. The low shooters will have an intense routine that's much more easy to copy and which will remain constant throughout the round.

You can tell at a distance whether a golfer is good or bad, even if you can't see how they're actually striking the ball. It's all in the way they approach their routine. One of the most obvious problems caused by a poor or ill-defined routine is the feeling of getting 'stuck' over the ball.

I stood one day and watched a large group of golfers tee off for a society match at Blackwood. Most of these folk were poor golfers and time and again I saw them do pretty much the same thing. They'd take a couple of nervous practice swings and then address the ball. Often they'd check their grip, or some other specific aspect of their stance, and then they'd wait. Then came a battle of wills with the ball, the golfers wanting to be very sure that by the time they actually hit the thing they had truly showed it who was boss. The trigger occurred not when they were ready but when they had deemed that the ball had been intimidated into submission. At this point they'd flail at the ball, which, of course, would immediately tip the balance of power back in its own favour. It would sail merrily into the trees, thereby showing the golfer who was really the boss.

Then a few low handicappers came along, and watching them was a totally different experience. I could tell their play was all target-based, and even if they weren't thinking about it logically, they were visualising the shot in some form. They made a couple of fluid practice swings, had a pause and a clear, focused look at the target, and then pulled the trigger. Their pre-shot routine taking much less time than the hacker's vague attempt at one.

For myself, I still didn't feel I had the whole process completely correct. I'd made my early breakthroughs with my modelling process and I continued to trawl the Internet, searching for examples of different swings. Each time Debbie told me to watch a particular aspect of my swing, I would video it, then paste it on my mobile and compare it to a perfect swing by somebody else. My favourites were Ernie Els, Retief Goosen, Nick Faldo, Ben Hogan (obviously, although it took a lot of digging to get a decent clip of his swing), and the old faithful from Jim McLellan. Every one a very good example of a classic swing.

Having absorbed their technique for a few days, I'd test my swing at the range. I'd measure twenty shots at the range with no pre-shot routine and then twenty with the routine in place. The difference in the quality of my shot-making was enormous. However, I still seemed unable to incorporate this properly into my play on the course. Late one evening, however, I was sitting, zombie-like, at the gym, feeling exhausted and watching the television, putting off the moment when I would begin my next round of exercise. I became aware that I was watching coverage of a tournament taking place in some far-off land. Pádraig Harrington was hitting a seven iron into the green. It landed inches from the hole and was just about the most perfect iron shot I'd ever seen. Absolutely effortless. It was such a beautifully controlled and compact swing that the image is burned into my brain for the rest of time.

A couple of days later I was out with Stuart, playing our usual match. I'd had what you might call a big night the previous evening and had only managed to get four hours' sleep. My head was pounding and the first six holes were catastrophic – I was seven over par and four down. Horrible golf. I stood on the tee facing disaster and humiliation. If I didn't get this together, it was going to be my biggest wipe-out of all our matches so far. I realised with a jolt that I needed to be able to deal with this type of situation if I was to stand a chance of getting my par round. I needed to dig deep into my bag of mental tricks and pull something out.

Then I remembered some advice I'd been given early in the challenge about breaking a round into three sets of six holes, as opposed to two sets of nine. I had a tendency to alter my golf after nine holes in a 'fresh start' kind of way. By treating it as three sets of six, I would gain an extra chance of a fresh start and wouldn't have to slog out so long waiting for the turn.

In my game with Stuart that day, I had a stern chat with myself and decided to use the seventh hole as my fresh start. We were playing at Bangor Golf Club, which is Stuart's home course, and the seventh is a par three of variable length. Today it was playing as a seven iron for me. I stood at the tee, took a deep breath to clear the cobwebs and imagined in intricate detail the Harrington shot I had seen a few nights before. I imagined that it was Harrington standing over the ball and I was standing several feet behind him. I then walked across and stepped into his body, as it were, and prepared to strike that very same shot. With this image playing in my mind, I went through my pre-shot routine and proceeded to hit one of the best shots of my life. It landed about a foot from the hole – as close to a hole in one as I have ever had.

This sparked off a complete transformation in my game. My mood perked up enormously and I proceeded to win the next seven holes in a row. It was a total vindication of just how effective visualisation and the pre-shot routine can be. What could have been a thrashing for me turned into a thrashing for Stuart instead. While I ploughed on relentlessly, his game fell apart. I knew that I was on to something.

Around the same time, I bought an old Ballesteros video on eBay. Seve's short game was the jewel in his crown, what really helped him win the big money. His video, *Short Game*, was inspirational, not from a technical perspective, but because of the sense of feel that he had. It harked back to a simpler era before the advent of gap wedges and lob wedges, and it was amazing to see how creative he was with his pitching and chipping, his incredible lightness of touch. Seve himself was, needless to say, delighted. The video would only work with the little portable TV which we kept in the bedroom, so with Lesley watching TV downstairs, Seve and I would sit side by side on the bed like Morecambe and Wise, watching it over and over.

Using my 'Harrington principle', I would imagine that I was Seve himself when I was chipping or pitching. I widened my stance a fraction and bent my knees a little more, and, like some daft eejit, I'd repeat 'Severiano Ballesteros' in a Spanish accent when I was pitching. Adulation and hero worship was moving to a new and slightly tragic level but, boy, was it effective. If there's one thing that Seve had in spades, it was confidence and self-belief. If I could transfer just an ounce of this to myself, it was bound to be of great benefit.

And through this new application of the visualising technique, my confidence in my short game went through the roof. Instead of merely visualising Seve beside me offering advice, it was almost as if I truly became Seve when I was playing in and around the greens.

Confidence and self-belief at a level far beyond mere mortals is the hallmark of most sporting geniuses, past and present. Ayrton Senna had it, Seve clearly had it and Jack Nicklaus had it, too. He was famed for his ability to play the back nine of the four majors with huge charges and displays of amazing aggressive golf. He seemed to be immune to the mental breakdowns that most golfers had under the intense pressure of these tournaments. A Nicklaus back-nine charge in a major was an awesome thing to behold and it was, he had always maintained, part of why he played golf.

There is a wonderful story about Nicklaus giving a speech to some students at his son's university. He was discussing his back nines with the students and maintained that he had never three-putted on the back nine of a major tournament on a Sunday. One student challenged him, saying that he had seen him do so. Nicklaus calmly repeated that he had 'never three-putted the back nine of a major tournament'. When the student replied that he had it on video for Nicklaus to see, the great golfer calmly repeated his statement, said there was no point in bringing in the video because it had never happened, and calmly moved on.

Such self-belief highlights a very important difference between 'them' and 'us', between those at the very highest levels of sport and those who are merely good at it. Golfing giants may have practised to a level where, physically, the shots become second nature, but they also have an unshakable belief in their ability and skill. Whether that be winning a major tournament or holing that tricky putt, it's a totally different mindset to the average good golfer, and a million miles away from the mindset of the average hacker fed a diet of 'this is how it works' by a low-teen handicapper who's been at it for years.

If you watch any brilliant putter before they take their stroke, their face is filled with total self-assurance and confidence. Just watch Tiger over those long putts, or Seve in his heyday. It's the same with any sport. Look at Ronaldinho before a free kick and you see that look. Watch Michael Jordan before a free throw. Wherever they got it from, that level of self-belief and target-based focus has to be at least as important as the quality of their stroke or kick or throw.

This self-belief was what I was after – it needed to last just long enough for me to get my one perfect round. It had lain dormant for many long years and now surfaced only occasionally to give me the lift I needed. The ability to ride this belief in myself and keep it steady and strong became as important for me as any other aspect of the game. In fact, the harnessing of self-belief was crucial to the whole challenge. I needed to be a Donald Trump or a Jack Nicklaus in my thinking, not some wee fella who would get battered down by a few low handicappers at Christmas.

A Virtual Boot Up the Ass

It has never been my object to record my dreams,
just to realize them.

MAN RAY

There is no doubt that these mental awakenings were helping my game. But, as I've said, golf is a lot more than just the mental game and I still needed to do a lot of physical work, particularly on my approach shots to the green. For research purposes, Dave Pelz's *Short Game Bible* was very useful. I'd tried to read this book in the early days of the challenge but found it too technical. Now, with a much greater understanding of the game, I took a second look at it.

Pelz has some very technical views about wedge use. His '3 x 4' wedge system, for example, illustrates that with four wedges, three set-strokes can be taken with each: a 7.30, 9.00 and 10.30-o'clock shot with each club, the time indicating the position of your left arm on the backswing, or your right arm if you're his left-handed star pupil Phil Mickelson. It's not a new system by any means. Many instructors use it under a different name. But Pelz's approach, in my opinion, is as good as it gets and is the most clearly presented.

The system enables you to create a chart of twelve distances, which can be replicated even in the heat of battle with some reasonable sense of confidence. It's a simple calculation and requires little 'feel' or creative input, which at times can be very useful. Obviously, it takes a bit of time to set up, because you need to hit a few dozen shots at every position in a wind-free environment to get your readings, but it is well worth the effort.

The process became a very useful part of my game and a great confidence booster. The 7.30 shot is tricky to replicate but the other two are very easy to repeat. I hold the view that from 50 yards and in, the game becomes a creative challenge again because there are more variables to deal with, but this process fills the gap between 50 and 100 yards very effectively.

So I adopted two radically different forms of short game. Around the green, I'd pull on the dark Slazenger clothes and white shoes and become Seve, but outside this zone and up to a full wedge I'd rely on Pelz's ultra-logical approach.

The interesting thing was that the distance figures I calculated were very similar to those I had worked out several months earlier when I first attempted to read *Short Game Bible*. If I could replicate them after several months away from the concept and without memory of the original distances, then it had to be a useful and accurate tool for the course.

I worked hard at this process and found it to be of great benefit. Initially, you need to do a fair amount of pacing to ensure that you have your distances right but, once happy with the results, you become very confident out on the course. I spent a lot of time on the par-three course at Blackwood, testing the system. I'd get used to pacing down from the 100-yard marker to get a good grasp of how many yards short of the green I was, and just do the sums based on the flag position that day. Once I had the distance, I'd look at my chart and simply select the club that most closely corresponded to it. Then all I had to do was dial it in and pull the trigger. For example, the third hole at Blackwood is a very short 68- or 80-yard hole, depending upon the tee position. It became a simple process of pulling out my sand wedge or gap wedge and dialling in 9.00 o'clock. No need to worry about having any 'feel' for the shot or how hard to hit the ball. Just pull out the club and pull the trigger.

Coupled with my Ballesteros process in my 50-yards-and-in game, this meant that my short game, apart from my putting, took a substantial leap forward. I was much more confident from 50 yards and out and was fluffing or ribbing far fewer chips and pitches round the green. Seve was working his confidence magic on me.

My putting, needless to say, continued to receive the sort of derisory contempt that I would give something I'd stepped on. I practised briefly on my putting mat and my putting stroke benefited to some extent. I kidded myself that I was working hard at it. But I wasn't.

The more I continued to develop the other parts of my game, the more I felt I could ignore my putting and just let my scoring improve through excellent driving and short game. Blackwood continued to suit my big drive and wedge game, so if I could get the ball close, I'd be able to putt from relatively short distances, without having to model myself on great putters like Ben Crenshaw or Brad Faxon. It's fair to say that this was bordering on self-deceit. I would tell myself, for example, that Ben Hogan was a master golfer, yet he wasn't a brilliant putter, that in fact, like me, he had a hatred of putting. As I continued to post my progress on the forum, some murmurings were surfacing about my emphasis on everything but putting. I was cocky and drunk with occasional success at this stage and put such trivial concerns out of my mind. Part of me genuinely believed that I could shoot par and still be a fairly mediocre putter. But it all came home to me in one terrible round at Blackwood.

It was now the end of February. I was playing with Stuart again and striking the ball beautifully. I hit two 330-yard drives (raise eyebrow, as necessary), which won Stuart's admiration.

'You're not driving the ball like a scratch player,' he said, 'you're driving like a professional.'

My iron play was also excellent, and yet I shot a 90. My short-game theory hadn't fully translated into decent results on the course by then, but more significantly, my putting performance was poorer than usual. It had actually regressed. I took a horrific eight three-putts! There are plenty of 24-handicappers out there who would putt infinitely better than that – any day of the week.

Once again my focus on achievement in certain aspects of my

game was causing me to ignore some fundamentals. There was no escaping it this time – I had to get better at putting.

That night I posted my progress on the Internet bulletin board and got an immediate response from one of the forum members who was usually blunt but supportive.

'Too many excuses not to practise your short game ... It makes you no different from the other hundreds of thousands of golfers out there who have a decent long game, but no idea what to do when they get to the green ...'

After my initial annoyance, his comment really struck home. He was absolutely right. I *was* like all the other golfers, getting caught up in the joy of the big drive.

It was the kick up the ass that I needed. For the next week I worked like a madman, gloriously gripped with total obsession once again, but at long last it was finally directed at my putting. I dug out my old Crenshaw and Faxon putting videos, and took the process right back to the basics. And I watched again the putting section on Seve's short-game video. Then, armed with all this information, I completely reworked my putting stroke, making it as simple and as easy to replicate as possible. Putting may well be ninety per cent 'feel', but if your basic mechanics are wrong, then you're still going to miss the hole. I incorporated a tiny forward press to stop me wavering about on the back stroke and then spent hours in practice.

I'd get up at the crack of dawn and spend an hour on my practice mat before breakfast. Every lunch time I'd wander round the course looking for empty greens and go through lots of drills, some from the videos and some that I invented myself. I'd practise long putts, short putts, 8-foot pressure putts, putting to tees placed in the green, putting to the fringe, playing billiards with other balls. Putting round a clock face, putting from 6 feet and forcing myself to start again every time I missed one. Evenings would be spent doing nothing but replicating my new stroke on the mat at home. Even when I sat in front of the television, I'd have the putter in my hand, to keep me comfortable with the feel of it. And finally, before I went to sleep, I'd visualise putting perfectly on every green at Blackwood.

Above all, Seve came to my rescue once more. I came across a very useful photograph of his hands gripping his old Ping putter, and when I replicated it, I was amazed at the lightness of the grip. So much so that I bought an old Ping putter just like Seve's to try to replicate the feeling even more. Sadly, I couldn't get comfortable with it, but as long as I'd mastered the grip that was all that mattered. And, as always, Seve stood quietly beside me as I putted away.

'Now you get eet, Mr Richardson. Now you understan'. Putting ees not a bad thing. Eet's a beautiful thing. Eet has a gentle feel and ees a wonderful game within the game. Forget the macho nonsense and start to love thees part of the game and you'll really make eet.'

By the end of the week, I'd spent a total of thirty-five hours concentrating on my putting, approximately thirty hours more than I'd done throughout the previous nine months. So did it pay off? Absolutely. Big time. I was a totally different putter by the end of it. My stroke was radically more predictable and my confidence levels had soared. I'd been *allowing* myself to be a bad putter and had told myself (and everyone else) so often that I was a bad putter that it had become a self-fulfilling prophecy. I'd even convinced myself that it wasn't really important. Now, through all of this hard graft, I could finally see that I *could* be a good putter.

It had been a sort of Psychology for Dummies session. Page One – Lesson One: 'Keep telling yourself that you're rubbish at something and don't be surprised if you are.' Even Stuart, who generally dismisses anything mental about the game of golf, would surprise me with his use of simple psychology to help him on the green. Standing over a 15-footer, he would regularly say things like: 'I don't miss many of these.' And lo and behold, into the hole it would drop. I doubt he was consciously thinking about the process, but it was certainly working for him all the same.

Obviously, belief in putting isn't something that you can just generate by a bit of positive thinking while watching *Coronation Street* and eating chips. My self-belief changed in the space of one week – as a result of the thirty-five hours of solid work. By any standards, though, that's not a huge amount of time to achieve something worthwhile. (Compare this to the fact that most of us waste an average of twenty-eight hours a week in front of the TV.)

The hard graft did a lot more than teach me good putting fundamentals, though. It made me feel that I *deserved* to be a good putter, that I had earned the privilege. And my next full round, exactly one week later on 6 March, was a blinder. My long game went off the boil a fraction, but I reduced my putting count from 40 to 28 and shot a 79. I had finally broken 80 again for the first time in nearly six months.

The process reminded me of something that had happened to me in my fifth-form year at school, during the run-up to my O-levels. We were in the middle of taking test exams to prepare us for the real thing, and I had a few days free before my next paper – the mechanics part of the mathematics course. I thought that I was half-decent at maths, but certainly no better; a fraction above the middle of the class, perhaps. In truth, I had little interest in the subject and didn't feel motivated to try to improve.

But on this occasion I decided, partly because I had a few days extra to study and partly because it was a relatively small part of my course, to work a little bit harder than usual. Additionally, this specific subject interested me in a way that other parts of the course didn't. Because it was a manageable amount of work, I was able to go over everything several times and suddenly realised that I grasped the whole concept with complete clarity. I reached a stage where there was no point in doing any more work because I already knew it.

I went into the exam with more confidence than I have had before or since, and I breezed it. I scored eighty-four per cent – a vastly better result than I had ever had in a maths exam – and I was comfortably at the top of the class. My maths teacher, of course, couldn't understand what had happened. But rather than taking me to one side to ask me about this remarkable improvement and how I'd achieved such a good result, he chose instead to accuse me of cheating in front of the whole class. I still remember my total indignation. I'm not going to blame him for future exam failures (although it might be convenient, and might appease my mother) but there is no doubt that knocks like this affect how children respond to success and failure. For a long time afterwards, I genuinely wondered what the point of working so hard was.

Relating this to golf, the vast majority of kids are not born with the God-given talent that Seve, Tiger or Nicklaus have. Most are just innocent, fragile wee creatures who take everything that their teachers and parents say as gospel. They are often forced into a 'respect your teacher above all' mentality, which I believe is a fundamentally flawed concept. Very few of my teachers actually deserved the respect that I was forced to give them, and I went to theoretically excellent schools. I can remember vividly the teachers who fired us up and gave us a bit of confidence; it was no coincidence that we would work particularly well for them.

Thankfully, most schools are different places these days, but the sort of 'toe the line' attitude at my school was a tremendously unhealthy environment for children to grow up in. It stifled original and unique thought and didn't give anyone a 'you can do it' attitude. A similar kind of negative attitude is often thrown at golfers who are actively trying to advance or improve their game by fellow golfers who are content with their mediocre game, or can't be bothered to even contemplate getting better. 'Don't expect miracles. Don't get carried away with any daft notions or newfangled ideas. It takes years to improve, you know!'

It was the reverse of this 'stick to the curriculum and take it steady' notion that I ultimately applied to my putting. I simply chose to change my perception of how hard putting was and how long I thought it would take for me to make a significant improvement. It was a microcosm of the whole year, really. I simply worked very hard in a short period of time and completely transformed my ability to putt.

It marked a serious turning point in my game and at long last a decent amount of self-belief started flowing back. I was shooting in the 70s again after the long winter, both on the par-three course and the full Hamilton course. I was regularly shooting seven or eight holes at level par or even one under. I planned to take a week off work in May to play at least once a day. In my private moments I believed I would shoot my level-par round that week and I'd be finished with time to spare.

I'd developed a very good swing and finally got on top of my short game. I was fit and my wrist and hips were relatively pain free. My grasp of the mental process was improving and I still had the guts of three months to complete the challenge. The momentum was flowing, my confidence was high and it seemed like only a matter of time ...

Martin Sheen and Guilt

To accomplish great things, we must dream as well
as act.

ANATOLE FRANCE

Of course, it's all very easy to go on about how we should all be
able to commit extra time to a task we love, but I'd be lying if
I said it didn't have an impact on my work colleagues and, more
importantly, on Lesley and Aimee. Finding thirty-five hours in
one intensive week to commit to my putting was difficult
enough to fit in with a busy job and family life but, as a one-off,
it was certainly possible. What was more consistently draining,
however, were the ten to twenty hours that I had to find for
practice week in and week out throughout the challenge. Giving up the box wasn't an issue for me, as I never watched a lot
of television anyway. The big problem was stealing away from
work and family life.

From a work perspective, I would try to nip up to the range
or the par-three course most lunch times. In the early days this
took little more than an hour. But later, I'd frequently get caught
up in my Zen-like state at the bottom of the range with Seve,
Hogan and the boys, and this hour would very quickly stretch
into an hour and a half, or even two, which was clearly pushing
my luck.

My other trick was to call into the range on the way back
from our garden centre in Bushmills for a quick 'twenty minutes'

of practice. But, for me, 'twenty minutes' on the range was the equivalent of 'a swift half' to an alcoholic, i.e. it never worked out that way. It used to take twenty minutes just to get warmed up and then I'd lose all sense of time. Before I knew it, I'd been at it an hour or more. Yet I spent the entire year in a state of denial about how much time I spent on practice.

I can remember a number of occasions when I was out on the course during the daytime, running round like a lunatic with a sickening feeling of guilt churning away inside me. I'd get a text from one of my fellow directors at the garden centre: 'Where R U?' I'd rush to the car, jump in and call back on my speaker phone.

'I'm just on my way back now. Sorry, I got a bit held up.'

'OK. It's just that they said you'd left Bushmills ages ago. We were wondering if you were all right.'

'Yep, yep, fine. I'll be there in ten minutes or so.'

So I avoided actually lying, but it always felt like a lie to me. I was abusing the trust and friendship of my partners and I felt guilty about it.

At home the guilt was even worse. Lesley was enormously supportive but I knew it was tough for her, especially in the evenings. I'd get home from work between six and seven and make sure I gave plenty of time to Aimee. We'd have dinner and then I'd read her a story and put her to bed. But it wasn't all plain sailing with Aimee either. It was difficult to make her fully understand why the house was littered with golf clubs and books. One night in October I was lying beside her at bedtime, reading *Harry Potter and the Chamber of Secrets*. (This was just at the start of her Harry Potter phase and we managed to get through the first five books that year.)

'Dad, why are you doing this golf thing?' she piped up, out of the blue.

'Well, you know the way I tell you that you can be anything you want if you just work hard enough?' I said, putting down the book.

'Yes, that I could become a famous actress or a pop star like Avril Lavigne if I wanted? Or even J.K. Rowling?'

'Yes, exactly. Well, when I was little, I decided that I wanted to become a professional golfer. I wanted to be like a man called Seve Ballesteros. You want to be like Avril – I wanted to be like Seve.'

'Ah, right, I see.'

'The problem was, I didn't stick at it. But I'm trying to stick at it now to see if I can play one really, really good round of golf in a year. Lots of people have told me it's not possible, so I'm working very hard to prove them wrong.'

'Right. So that's why you do all those stupid swings in front of a mirror?'

'Er, yes.'

'And that's why you leave all the mess about and make lots of noise with your practising when I'm trying to get to sleep.'

'Well, kinda, yes.'

I wasn't exactly happy with how my little motivational speech was going.

'And that's why Mum got so cross and used the s-word when she tripped up on your mat the other day.'

I winced. 'I suppose.' This wasn't going the right way at all.

'And that's why you did that *stupid* and embarrassing swinging when we were in Tesco and the lady in the queue looked at you like you were a bit mad?'

She smirked, knowing she had me, and fluttered her eyelashes like a teenager.

Here was I giving a pep talk to my seven-year-old and she was managing to make a fool out of me. I laughed.

'Well – yes. That's all correct and I know that it's actually very annoying for you and Mum at times, but it's just one of those things I have to do.'

'Yeah, yeah, I know. But – when will you be finished?'

'May.'

There was a pause.

'When's May again?'

'After April.'

'Right. And when's April?'

'Next year. After March.'

'Next year!' She was aghast. 'You mean, I have to put up with you doing embarrassing swings until *next year*?'

''Fraid so, sweetheart.'

She sighed and rolled her eyes.

'Right. Can we get back to the book now?'

I was far from convinced I'd got my case across to her at all.

In March I really started to turn up the heat. I had several days where I was hitting more than five hundred balls in practice and the par-three course became my regular lunch-time haunt. As long as it was quiet, I could run around and play the eighteen holes in about an hour.

I was reading Nick Faldo's autobiography at this stage and it made me even more determined to succeed. I clearly remembered – from when I was younger – Faldo becoming the golden boy of golf and then disappearing off the scene as he changed his swing. Superficially this seemed like madness and, like Tiger when he made his big swing change, the press (and the sponsors who dropped him) let him know what they thought.

But Faldo's quiet determination and relentless belief kept him going. His work rate was epic, and the fifteen hundred balls he hit in one day dwarfed the five hundred or so that I was hitting on my best days. Reading about Faldo's achievements helped me shift to a different plane in terms of attitude. To the average golfer, five hundred balls a day is almost inconceivable – most wouldn't hit that number a year in practice – but to folk like Faldo, Tiger or Hogan it's nothing. They have, through circumstance, genetics, experience or some other factor, managed to look at improvement in a very different way. Once more it became crystal clear that I needed to ignore classic amateur golfer thoughts and to try to tap into my inner Faldo.

Faldo's work ethic yielded remarkable results. Once his new swing was in place he made it to the very top. He was world number one for ninety eight weeks, won three British Opens, three Masters and was arguably the most successful European golfer of all time. His relationship with the press never improved but his almost solitary, single-minded attitude created an indomitable force out on the course. At this stage in my challenge, Faldo's attitude was as important a lesson as his ability to work incredibly hard at his game.

I kept up with my short game and putting practice. I tried to keep it simple; I didn't want to be learning any new shots or techniques. I was aware that my swing, good as it was, could easily move out of kilter. I've watched many low handicappers with, on the face of it, much worse swings than mine hit the ball with greater consistency, mainly because they were happy and comfortable in their own swing. They had reached a stage where they knew their swing wasn't perfect but they had some decent compensatory actions, and when things went wrong, there were just one or two known variables they could work on.

If I wasn't careful, my swing, because it was so new and fresh, could get out of sync in lots of different ways and it would take me a week or so to grasp fully what was going on. Foolishly, I'd become stubborn again about asking Debbie for help. I felt I'd read so much and learned so much that I should have been able to resolve these issues myself. A mistake. Debbie knew my swing so well by now that five minutes with her could save me hours, even days, of thrashing about trying to solve the problem myself.

Every evening, after I put Aimee to bed, I was itching to get back up to the range again. I'd fidget about downstairs, asking Lesley a few questions about her day that she knew I wasn't really interested in. Then I'd maybe check my e-mails, and eventually ask was it all right to head off again. The answer, to her eternal credit, was always yes. Even on those occasions when I was struggling with motivation and actually looking for an excuse not to go, she never gave me one. She never said, 'Please don't go up tonight, I need you to do something or other in the house.' She never said, 'Please don't go up tonight, you've worked really hard at it and deserve a break.' She never said, 'Please don't go up tonight because I'm thoroughly pissed off,' – even though she would admit much later that she wanted to, many times. This support was enormously important to me and certainly made the whole process a lot easier.

I gratefully accepted Lesley's generosity and support but I'd frequently feel a wave of guilt crash over me as I left the house.

I was making time for Aimee but much less so for Lesley. I think if it hadn't been for Martin Sheen and *The West Wing*, my guilt would have been much worse. Lesley was a huge fan of the show but had only seen the first three seasons. By a great stroke of luck we discovered early on in my year that the fourth season could be rented from Amazon. But such was Lesley's passion for the fictional American president and his dynamic entourage that she decided to go back to the beginning. So we rented the first four seasons, which eventually turned into five seasons, and then six (and has, as I write, become seven). She would sit at home and watch *The West Wing* and I'd drift off again up to the range for more practice. If I had to leave her alone night after night with another man, then I was happy enough with her choice of Martin Sheen (the other option was Des Lynam, but that's another story!), and I often wondered if he was providing counsel for her the way Seve was for me. She certainly knows an awful lot more about the American political system than I ever will. On the rare occasions when I was at home in front of the box, I was never quietly snuggled up on the sofa with her. Oh no. It was either watching a golf DVD in the next room or sitting in bed with Seve, watching his short-game video.

Of course, it didn't just stop there. There was also the regular game of golf on Sunday mornings with Stuart and a couple of stolen sessions on Saturdays. And there were the countless magazines and books lying around the house, as well as dozens of gadgets that I was rapidly accumulating to help me deal with certain aspects of my swing. Lesley was forming a firm friendship with the postman who was delivering all this stuff almost on a daily basis. Then there were the broken light shades and scuffs on the wooden floors where I'd practise my chipping. There was the putting mat to trip over and tees to stand on and balls rolling around every room in the house. Putting up with the debris from this obsession of mine became Lesley's own challenge.

During the long summer nights, I'd seldom be back before ten-thirty. I'd stay as long as light permitted, and often eked out my practice session well into dusk. One night there was a particularly bright full moon and I was chipping and pitching to the sixth hole, totally lost in my own world. I happened to glance at my watch, and nearly choked. It was after midnight! Surprised that Lesley hadn't phoned to see where I was, I delved into my pocket, looking for my mobile, and realised with a sinking feeling that it wasn't there. Shit. Perhaps I'd left it in the car. I scurried back to the car park, aware that Lesley would probably be going berserk, and jumped into the car. No phone. Double shit. Driving home like a madman, I knew I was in big trouble.

Lesley was standing in the living room in a terrible state, phone in her hand, about to call the police.

'Don't you ever, ever, do that to me again,' she screamed, tears running down her face. 'I thought a poacher had shot you, or that you'd had a heart attack somewhere on the course or had been in a car accident.'

As I consoled her, I saw my mobile sitting on the table. It was switched off. When I turned it on, there were seventeen missed calls – all from Lesley. Needless to say, my guiltometer went through the roof. I set myself an 11 p.m. curfew, and never forgot my phone again.

Dreams Sometimes Have Repercussions

> Change is the law of life. And those who look only
> to the past or present are certain to miss the future.
>
> JOHN F. KENNEDY

The goal had always been to pursue this challenge within certain criteria. When Tony and I first dreamed up the Big Idea all those years ago, we knew there needed to be a few provisos. In essence, the challenger had to be someone that people could relate to. A 'real' person, someone with normal social constraints – someone with a job, a family, everyday responsibilities. I fitted the bill perfectly and the goal became winning the challenge without jeopardising either my marriage or my job.

But any challenge like this one cannot fail to change your perceptions of life. It is impossible to expose yourself to something as intense as realising an 'impossible dream' without being forced to change your thinking about how you live your life. Something was going to have to change when it was all over, and I was determined that the something wasn't going to be my marriage.

I was becoming increasingly disillusioned with my working environment and was having serious doubts about staying in the garden-centre business. What had started out as an exciting adventure and a dream in itself – to expand the business to five garden centres as quickly as possible – had begun to change. As directors, we all had differing requirements and this, coupled with a slight shift in the marketplace meant that we were becoming a little direction-less. We had consolidated at two centres rather than continuing to grow to the five we had dreamed of and I believed that the business would stagnate as a result. But, as only one of four directors, I felt powerless to change this state of affairs.

So, for the first time in my life, I was dealing with the politics of running a larger business rather than winging it with the seat-of-my-pants entrepreneurial stuff I was used to. I didn't like it, it wasn't my style, and I wasn't good at it.

If there's one thing I am good at, however, it's getting out of situations that I don't like. I have this life's-too-short clock ticking away inches from my face at all times, and I hate getting caught up in situations where I feel I'm just drifting. So, finally, after weeks of growing unease, I made a decision. I was going to leave the business.

In April I sat down with my fellow directors and explained how I felt. The timing was awful and it would be fair to say they weren't pleased. They had been very supportive of me throughout the year, after all, and even though we employed more than a hundred staff, ours was a tight-knit business. It looked like I was running away because thing weren't going my way. But that wasn't the case. I simply felt unable to work within the new structure that was evolving in the business. You can change some parts of your personality to fit the environment, but if you change too much, you become ineffective and I could already feel that happening to me. I wasn't doing as good a job as I should, and that wasn't benefiting anyone.

My decision didn't go down well at home, either. Understandably. I'd spent the best part of a year creating chaos in the house and disappearing off to the range every night, and now I'd decided to give up our main source of income. It seemed like the actions of a lunatic or, perhaps more accurately, a selfish prick. Lesley never said this in so many words, but that's what I felt like.

That weekend the three of us were due to go to Portsalon in County Donegal with Stuart and his fiancée, Maeve. I hoped the break would give Lesley and me a chance to think things through. No deal had been struck as yet with my co-directors regarding my shares and the terms of how and when I would leave, so I needed a bit of space to take stock, think clearly about what I was doing and why I was doing it.

The atmosphere in the car on the way up was strained. And yet, despite the fact that I knew I was acting selfishly, I could feel a weight being lifted off my shoulders. As soon as we arrived at the beautiful cottage, which is owned by Stuart's stepfather, Maeve took Lesley and Aimee horse riding, and Stuart and I went to play a round of golf. Out on the course I told him of my plan. He thought I'd gone mad. He was so annoyed that he walked off down the fairway in front of me, shaking his head and muttering. He'd been nothing less than completely supportive during the past months, but now he felt he needed to do something to halt what he perceived to be a moment of insanity on my part.

Throughout the rest of the round, he tried to come up with all sorts of ways to persuade me to at least wait until the challenge was over before making a final decision. I knew what he was thinking. Perhaps my game would go off the boil again and the 'dream' would turn into a nightmare. I'd end up with a huge amount of egg on my face and no income. I was either having a complete mental breakdown or an absurd midlife crisis. Despite my conviction that I was doing the right thing, I found it difficult to come up with a coherent argument against him.

That night we sat in the lovely cottage, perched on a small cliff top, and admired the stunning views. Stuart cooked some exceptional fillet of beef and provided some very fine burgundy. But the tense atmosphere was still there, and as we sat at the table my decision was pored over and analysed by Lesley, Stuart and Maeve.

'Could you not do a deal to keep the coffee shop at the garden centre?' said Lesley.

'Would you not just give it until the end of the year?' This was Stuart.

'Couldn't you try to change things at the centres to create an environment that would suit you?' said Maeve.

All valid and reasonable questions, which offered some potential solutions. But I knew none of them would work. The coffee shop was a wonderful operation, with some really great staff, and my main skill and interest was in that side of the business. I would have loved to have kept it. But I knew it wouldn't be a workable scenario. The others wouldn't want to sell it to me for a start, and a clean break was probably better for everyone.

The evening wore on and I suddenly felt exhausted by it all. So I excused myself and went to bed.

The others talked on late into the night. Lesley was deeply concerned. I'd provided one too many roller-coaster rides for her during our marriage and the novelty had worn thin. Stuart was still incredulous. He confided in Lesley that he was having serious doubts that I would actually make it. And who could argue with him? That day I'd failed to break 80. I'd scored no better than a 9 or a 10-handicapper and that was a long way away from where I needed to be. The Johnnie Boy Book of Golfing Excuses had managed to notch this down to the fact that I was playing a tough, unfamiliar course while trying to field Stuart's probing enquiries into my plan to leave work.

Upstairs, despite my exhaustion, I lay awake on the bed. It was a clear, cloudless night and I left the curtain open a little to watch the moon shining on the still water below. I could hear them talking downstairs but thankfully not the specifics of what they were saying. I knew the gist of it, though.

A wave of self-doubt suddenly hit me. What exactly was I doing? Perhaps this was an unattainable dream. Was Sam Torrance right after all? Maybe I needed to wake up to reality. The fear of failing the challenge and a sudden panic at perhaps not being able to pay the mortgage gripped me hard. Was I going to become one of those bitter, penniless dreamers who end up with nothing concrete to show for themselves in their old age? I drifted off into a restless sleep, but the following morning woke with a steely determination to stick to my guns. Deep down in my heart I knew I had made the right decision and gradually, after talking it through once more, Lesley accepted that I had to do it.

The following week I resumed my negotiations with my fellow shareholders. We looked at various options and finally arrived at a very fair price for my shares and agreed that I would leave in three months.

So, by the middle of July, I would be out of work. Technically, I would have fulfilled my criteria of still being in work at the end of the challenge, but only by the skin of my teeth. And, despite my earlier high spirits and seemingly boundless confidence, I had to face the fact that there were no guarantees I would complete the challenge successfully.

The Power of Possibilities

We need men who can dream of things that never
were.

JOHN F. KENNEDY

With only a couple of months to go, most of the members of
the golf forum were giving me every encouragement, and the
advice I was getting was generally very useful. The nay-sayers
and their gloomy predictions had dropped off and I was left with
some solid and excellent support.

I had also managed to find a real-life, albeit Internet-based,
mastermind group to complement my bunch of imaginary
famous friends. This eclectic gang included an Internet special-
ist from Germany, a music producer from Los Angeles and a
Dublin-based entrepreneur. They applauded my successes and
spurred me back into action when I was slacking or getting
bogged down in some 'it's so hard' self-pity. And they helped me
keep some balance when I was getting ahead of myself, or when
I was in danger of being beaten down by too many negative
comments.

Among the golfing fraternity on the Internet forum a fierce
debate erupted over the percentage of golfers who can, or
cannot, make it to scratch. This time, the argument wasn't
directed at me, but the thinking fascinated me and highlighted
some of the issues I'd faced during the challenge.

Certain keyboard warriors still had a dig from time to time at my progress. They seemed to enjoy telling me I was still a million miles away from succeeding at the challenge – 'Sorry mate, you have no chance. If you're only shooting X at this stage, you should give up.' There are a number of generally accepted truths in golf. One is that it's much easier to take ten shots off your game if you're a 100-shooter than it is if you're an 80-shooter. There is some merit to this argument, but it's yet another of those myths that prevent golfers from making big progress, and it holds them back on the course.

These truths do not solely prevail online; they are just as common at golf clubs. Club golfers form cliques like gangs of kids at school. The cool kids have low handicaps and great booming drives. A few who lack the booming drives but have great scrambling skills are allowed in the clique, too. And a final group are allowed in because they have money, and are prepared to pay for drinks and sponsor competitions. Just like at school, what these guys say is taken as gospel. Most of the really good golfers, who play off scratch or who are plus-1 or plus-2 markers, don't have time for this nonsense, so the advice within the clique is from the single-figure gang. While clearly good golfers, this crowd perpetuates golfing myths. Few of them go in for lengthy and disciplined sessions on the range, preferring to grind it out on the course, relying on a grooved-in swing and a competitive attitude to get them through.

The attitudes of this gang are treated as gospel by any new players. The beginners become like fleas who learn not to jump too high because the lid is there. They learn to accept the lid and play hard for a few years in order to join the gang. Just like school, it's easier to join them than to do your own thing.

My friend Mark McMurray, who inspired the challenge, was regarded as slightly mad, both for his behaviour and for the goals that he set himself. Rather than adjourning to the clubhouse when he finished a round, he would do some extra practise instead. He was variously distrusted and dismissed for failing to engage in any of the club's rituals. To a certain extent I had the same experience. 'You'll not learn it on the range' was a favourite refrain of lots of club regulars, and I'm sure there were plenty more such comments that were said out of my earshot.

The Internet differs because users don't have to talk and whisper behind closed doors. Discussions can become very aggressive very quickly – with anonymity protected by a daft user name and, often, several thousand miles, users can be as rude as they like and revert to school bully-type behaviour.

Bored with these Internet wrangles, I played safe and said that maybe only eighty to ninety per cent of golfers can achieve this (even though I actually believe that all golfers can). Unfortunately, this didn't deter one poor soul who, unfamiliar with Internet playground games, was relentless in his assertion that anyone could play off scratch. It was like a fox getting caught by a pack of hounds. After some terrible verbal abuse, he deleted all of his postings and never returned to the forum again.

Such hounding of a person, merely for holding a belief in the possibility of a thing, is deeply unpleasant to witness. How can some people be so blinkered by their own beliefs that they refuse to accept that others may not think the same way? The golfing fraternity does seem to have more than its fair share of these gloomy pessimists. And it's hard to watch new golfers being held back by their more experienced brothers, when they should instead be receiving encouragement to reach their full potential. Being persuaded that something is beyond the realms of possibility, even before an attempt has been made, is such a tragic waste of potential talent. I'd urge new players not to follow the herd, don't take what the majority says as gospel, and follow your own dream.

Sometimes, you just have to tell yourself that you *can* do a thing. Here's a good exercise. If you are trying to get better at golf, then sit down quietly somewhere and say out loud, 'I can play a level-par round.' Then just let the statement hang there. Try not to think of anything in particular, and listen to what goes on inside your head. Very quickly your inner voice will pipe up with the reasons why you can't play to par.

'You're way too old, mate.'

'Sure, how on earth could you practise that much?'

'Ah, but your clubs are rubbish – nobody could ever shoot par with those things.'

'But you have an odd swing. You'll never be able to swing like a scratch golfer.'

'Naah. You couldn't afford the lessons.'

'You simply can't take the time off work.'

'There is absolutely no way your wife/husband would ever let you out that much. No chance.'

The list could be endless, but as long as you come up with some rational reasons for not going ahead, then you have something to work on.

If it's the quality of your equipment you're worried about, then you can dismiss that pretty quickly just by considering the equipment that Bobby Jones used three-quarters of a century ago, and comparing that with your theoretically 'inferior' gear.

If you feel that you can't practise enough, then try to work out ways to practise more. Give up five hours' television a week, or take a few lunch breaks at the range.

And if you can't afford the cost of the practice balls, then work out what you could give up instead. A couple of hundred balls at the range, for example, might cost the same as a couple of pints of beer.

Whatever your negative responses are, and almost inevitably they will be negative to begin with, just slowly and rationally think through the process as if you were offering advice to a child or a teenager who viewed you as a wise elder or mentor. You don't even need to have a fictional Hogan or Seve beside you. All you need to do is listen to the *positive* voice in your head and it will start to counter the negative arguments in an equally rational and reasonable manner. Just keep asking the questions and keep probing for honest answers.

After you have your first set of answers, you should dig a little deeper to see what else might lie there. Ultimately, you'll end up with the *true* reason why you don't want to get better. You might say to yourself: 'I could play a level-par round if I gave up going out for a drink with the mates on Wednesdays and practised more.' Dig a little deeper and other issues may be revealed.

Concerns about not being accepted by your friends so much, or even worries that beating them on the course could lead to unpopularity.

Whatever the reasons, the answers do lie within yourself. You don't need a psychiatrist to probe and analyse why you are resisting, you just need to ask the right questions. In the end, you may decide that a decent plan of improvement isn't right for you and that's fine. Undoubtedly, sacrifices have to be made and that may not be for everybody. But do make sure that your decision has not been unduly influenced by the negative opinions of others. Be sure it is your own view, which has been reached by your own inner debate, and if that is the case, then don't force it on other golfers.

Sadly, most people will never take the time to do this simple exercise, lift their barriers and have a man-to-man (or woman-to-woman) chat with themselves. A shame, really, as the technique can clearly be extended beyond golf. It's an excellent way of establishing why you don't want to go for a promotion, change jobs, learn a language, start a business, or any of the many 'tough' things that we have to do or choose between. It allows you to get a much better idea of what it is that is actually holding you back. An immensely useful process. Trust me.

The Golfer's Thermostat

It is not the critic who counts ... The credit belongs
to the man who is actually in the arena.

THEODORE ROOSEVELT

At this stage in the challenge I became convinced of the concept
that golfers have a handicap thermostat. A thermostat based not
on their ultimate ability, but on two key factors – their recent
handicap and the handicaps of the golfers they play with.

A simple test will prove my point. Add up your handicap for
the past five years and divide it by five. Next, add up the five
handicaps of the five golfers you most regularly play with and
divide this figure by five. Now add these two figures together
and divide them by two. I have found that in nearly ninety per
cent of cases this figure will be within two strokes of your
current handicap.

A golfer's handicap is based almost entirely upon past performance and the performance of those people around him. This
makes it extremely difficult for the average club golfer to make
a big bid for single-figure freedom if he's, say, a 14-handicapper,
simply because it will upset this applecart.

So ask yourself, do I want to stay at the same level? Most
golfers will answer that they really do want to play better,
although they never actually do anything about it. It is a wish and
not an intention. If you truly intend to get better, then you will
actively seek ways to achieve that goal.

Play around with this notion and see how it feels. See how your inner voice deals with the situation. Let's assume you have the average club golfer's handicap of 17. Now, imagine you had a handicap of 5 and see how this makes you feel. Initially, you may feel that this would be wonderful. You'd be able to beat your buddies and vastly cut down on the balls you lose. You'd have a repeatable swing that would look good, rather than your current swipe. But now, think a little deeper. In all likelihood, you'd be asked to play in a variety of club competitions; you'd be under pressure to perform in challenging games with excellent golfers you don't know or maybe don't like. You'd be forced to commit time to practice and wouldn't be able to goof around so much on the course. Would it really be as much fun? You'd have to cancel some of your regular four-ball games to spend time playing with the big boys. If any part of this scenario makes you feel uncomfortable, then they are the issues that you need to deal with.

It might help if you were to ease up on the aspiration and take your fictional future handicap to 10 and see how that feels. Perhaps that's a level you'd be more comfortable with. You'd still be the best guy in your group but you wouldn't have totally ostracised yourself. If that still feels too much, then what about 12? How does that feel? If 12 feels good on all levels, then change this aspiration from being a wish to an intention. Make it a clearly articulated goal with a deadline. And, of course, have a plan. It won't be easy, but within a relatively short period of time, with a sequence of lessons and a decent level of concentration on the short game, a 12 handicap is well within the reach of most golfers. Any golfer, at any level, can use this process to improve his or her game. It's all about who we associate with and what we actually intend to *do* as opposed to *wish for*.

Even at a professional level, golfers can lower their sights when faced with a seemingly invincible opponent. Take what happened when Tiger Woods came along. It was universally acknowledged among many of the best golfers in the world that when Tiger would start a tournament there was a sense of simply playing for second best. Practically speaking, they'd given up even before the tournament had started.

During my challenge year, Tiger's crown had slipped slightly. He was in a process of changing his swing and hadn't won a major tournament for a couple of years. The Internet was inundated with faceless goons proclaiming that he was all washed up, his career over. It all reminded me of what Theodore Roosevelt once said:

> It is not the critic who counts; not the man who points out how the strong man stumbles, or where the doer of deeds could have done them better. The credit belongs to the man who is actually in the arena, whose face is marred by dust and sweat and blood, who strives valiantly; who errs and comes short again and again; because there is no effort without error and shortcomings; but who does actually strive to do the deeds; who knows the great enthusiasm, the great devotion, who spends himself in a worthy cause, who at the best knows in the end the triumph of high achievement and who at the worst, if he fails, at least he fails while daring greatly. So that his place shall never be with those cold and timid souls who know neither victory nor defeat.

I could imagine Tiger smiling confidently at all those who felt they could criticise him, then calmly turning back to his practice. He did, of course, survive this brief slump and dominates the world of golf once more. I printed out the wonderful Roosevelt quote and put it on the notice board above my desk at home. And there it remains – one of the most inspiring speeches I've ever come across.

I became fascinated by the psychology of how we improve. I was in a unique position to observe the golfing world and not get sucked into the standard model of improvement. Talking about the challenge one day, a friend and I tried to extrapolate the level that I might have been playing at if I'd stuck at it all those years ago. We concluded that I would have probably been around the 13-handicap mark. That would have slotted me into the middle/upper zone of those friends of mine who were regular golfers.

And it is likely that I'd have had exactly the same attitude to improvement as ninety per cent of golfers have at this level. I'd have sat in the bar and moaned about my putting, about how a local PGA pro was useless, and about how hard it all was. I'd have listened earnestly as my 12-handicap friend offered advice on my swing, based on an article he had read sitting over breakfast that very morning. Then I'd have bought another round of drinks and wasted another hour. I'd never have contemplated spending that money, or that time, on a half-hour lesson instead.

Approaching the game from the perspective of the challenge offered me an entirely different way of thinking. My attitude to improvement was based on my experience in business and the huge golfing improvements that people like Mark McMurray had achieved in the past. This doesn't mean I was totally untainted or unaffected by general golfing attitudes, but the challenge certainly put me in an unusual position, which I found was very beneficial.

I became curious about my own psychological drives. I wanted to discover what buttons I needed to press to get me through this thing. I still had regular periods of frenzied activity at the range, when I had to hide my car from Debbie, but I also had periods when I really couldn't be bothered any more.

The timing of my challenge year was once again proving to be a problem. With the hectic spring and early summer period almost upon us, all hands had to be on deck at the garden centres. To prepare for this onslaught, March is an especially busy time. Of course, this clashed with my challenge dates. Just when I needed to be cranking up my golf practice, I also needed to be grafting harder than ever at work.

We had a strict no-holiday rule during the three months of April, May and June, which applied to staff and directors alike. I had planned to abuse this rule by taking a week off in May, which made it even more difficult to steal some practice time in this period.

My business partners continued to be very tolerant, but ultimately I still had a job to do. Undoubtedly, my absences were creating staffing problems and my golf, to an outsider, must have seemed a frivolous challenge. I couldn't blame them for think-ing it was all becoming a bit of a nuisance. I knew I was pushing my luck but the obsession and the dream kept driving me on.

On top of this, the weather had changed for the worse and my arthritis was playing up again. I bought a heat lamp and dosed myself with glucosamine and cod liver oil. I started wearing a Sabona copper bracelet, just like Seve, which, in my Walter Mitty imagination, helped me get a tiny step closer to the great man just by looking down at my wrist. I'd lie on the sofa with the lamp directed at my hips and wrist every night and visualise my way round the course.

I hadn't yet managed to climb out of that dark well of anxiety and self-doubt. With work and various social events coming up, problems surfaced to prevent me getting out there, yet this was the stage, more than any other, when I needed to be devoting maximum time to the challenge.

Motivation to push that bit harder and an understanding of what made me tick were more important than ever. There are basically two forms of motivation – the stick you move away from and the carrot you move towards or, as the motivational guys describe them, pain and pleasure.

In my current scenario, pleasure would derive from the joy of standing on the eighteenth hole sinking the putt for a level-par 71. It would come from my deep sense of satisfaction and the congratulations of my friends and family. Yes, pleasure was all about standing like Rocky at the end of his fight with Apollo Creed – bloodied but victorious. It was about a mad, jumping hug from Seve and his brothers, just like he got after his first Open Championship in 1979, and it was about a respectful handshake and a 'Fair play, mate' from Sam Torrance. A couple of pints of Guinness with Darren Clarke and a big, smiling slap on the back were there in the mix, too.

The other side of the coin was pain, the pain I had to move away from. I had always felt that the successful completion of my challenge would bring about a life change. The possibility of reinventing myself. I had taken the first step – I had negotiated my exit from the business and my new life was waiting to begin in July. The thought of all this falling through, of suffering the pain of failure and the ridicule of all those nay-sayers, would be enough to jettison me from the sofa on a rainy night and kick me out the door for a lengthy practice session. That was a stronger motivator than all the praise and backslapping I could ever dream of.

So, for my motivation, I chose to poke myself with the stick at least as much as I dangled the carrot in front of my eyes. If all you focus on in golf is removing the pain of that horrible slice you've been having, then that's all you'll achieve. If you genuinely have made a plan for improvement, a solid intention and not a wish, then you can use both these types of motivation to spur yourself on to action. Different things will work on different days, depending upon your mindset, but at the very least it provides you with a couple of options to get you off the sofa or out of the bar. You can mentally scroll through a menu of options that you know have got you moving in the past.

And there are always things you can do even if you have a genuine excuse not to practise. With the ever-present problems in my wrist, I became hugely proficient in playing with one hand. I'd swing away and work on my 'feel'. And as very little body movement is essential to strike a ball cleanly with one hand, this practice, in turn, helped to sort out my 'Elvis legs'. I could also pitch, chip and putt, without causing too much pain and inflammation.

As April progressed, it didn't matter whether the motivator button was carrot or stick, hugs or Guinness, or just the burning desire to stick two fingers up to the doubters – what I needed was to keep going. It was a whatever-it-takes moment.

Knights in Shining Armour

> Those who dream by day are cognizant of many things which escape those who dream only by night.
>
> EDGAR ALLAN POE

It was all lining up. The weather was improving, I was playing well again and concentrating on all parts of my game. I'd finally sorted my putting and I had my week off work coming up before too long. I knew I should be trying to play with some better golfers in an effort to see what shortcomings there were in my game, but I knew very few single-figure handicappers.

Towards the end of March, in search of some inspiration and a little bit of last-minute direction, I'd picked up the phone and rung Mark McMurray. I knew he hadn't been playing much because he was also suffering badly from arthritic hips but I wanted to ask if there was any chance he might go out with me and play a few holes. I needed somebody at his level to tell me what I was doing wrong or at least give me some pointers to work towards.

Despite his arthritis, he willingly agreed. So out we went one April evening, with Stuart along for the ride. An inspirational and eye-opening ride it was, too.

My game was OK and I was easily keeping up with or out-driving Mark, but the difference in his touch and mine around the green was like chalk and cheese. On countless occasions I hit a drive at least as good as his and yet by the time we marked the card he always seemed to be a shot less than me.

A magical touch with a wedge was what made the difference. I believed I had become pretty hot in this area but the difference was a yawning chasm. It was also one of those rounds where I became frustrated with myself early on for not 'showing what I can do', as Stuart put it. I shot about an 80 but with fairly scrappy golf. I didn't believe it was going to inspire Mark with any real confidence that I could win the challenge, but he knew exactly what I was thinking. He remembered that feeling so well, he said. The frustration of knowing that you can play well and yet being unable to perform in front of the very people who are there to gauge your level of improvement. It had affected me many times over the past months and would cause me even greater problems in the immediate future.

Mark strongly advised me to concentrate fully on my short game and keep at it. So I duly worked like a madman on my short game once more. Mark had done those little pitches that bounce once and then stop dead, just like the pros on television. It's a showman shot but that was the type of control I was desperate for. That was the gap I had to close in the next few weeks and I was determined to do everything in my power to ensure that I would close it.

Mark had also noticed a couple of things about my swing with my driver that made him feel my club wasn't quite right. A few days later he called me to say he had a club for me. It was an R510 TP with a Fujikura Six extra stiff shaft in it. That's a ludicrous amount of jargon for a full tour-spec club that cost in the region of £400. The shaft seemed extremely stiff to me but he told me to give it a try, guaranteeing that I'd hit my drives a bit straighter. And he was absolutely right. I lost a little distance but my drives were much more accurate. He wouldn't accept a penny for the club and I was very touched by the gesture.

I'm often struck by the way people come to your aid when they see you stick your neck out. I had received a lot of free help during the year and would again over the next few weeks.

Without this, I simply wouldn't have made all the progress in the game that I ultimately made.

Late one night, when I was drifting round the Internet looking at golf articles, I came across the website of Dr Carey Mumford. I had visited his site before, when a forum member had recommended his work, but at that time I didn't feel ready to cope with the intricacies of Carey's views on golfing mental processes. To be honest, much of what he said had sailed over my little Irish head. But now I was at a different stage.

I got in touch with him and he was supportive of my challenge and keen to help. As much as anything else, Carey likes a doer, and he was impressed with me putting myself on the line and giving it a shot.

I'm doing Carey a disservice by simplifying his process too much but, at its most basic, the golfer is encouraged to come up with a phrase, or 'clear-key', which will help to clear his mind during his swing. It was similar to Gallwey's idea in *The Inner Game of Golf*, but Carey dealt with it in much greater detail and, I thought, offered a more usable system. It also seemed to be a logical extension of the anchoring process I had been using in my pre-shot routine.

With Carey's system, you go through your normal pre-shot routine and then when you stand over the ball, you start to repeat a phrase that is totally unrelated to golf. As you begin to utter the phrase, you start the swing. Your mind cannot accommodate a swing thought or anything that might ruin the stroke if you say the phrase with a reasonable amount of conviction. If you're brave enough, you can even say it out loud. People have used various assertions, such as 'beautiful swing', in an effort to invoke a positive feeling during the swing. Carey, however, argues that this is an unhelpful approach. The phrase, he insists, must be unrelated to golf.

I experimented with a number of phrases before I came up with one that worked. Some phrases have a logical pause halfway through and you can easily slot a swing thought into it and muck the whole process up. For example, take 'Ayrton Senna was the greatest', which was my original choice. This seemed to have a slight pause right after 'Senna', just at the point when I was making contact with the ball. I settled on 'Three-hundred-and-fifty-eight million' because it flowed without a pause. The fact that it was a number, too – something abstract – helped to clear my mind of any aspect of the swing.

My pre-shot routine now looked like this:

- Stand behind the ball and start the visualisation process.
- Walk over the commit line and twizzle the club at the target while repeating 'incredible' and dragging back the euphoric feeling with a smile.
- Two practice swings with an emphasis on a perfect follow-through and then stand over the ball still repeating 'incredible' and visualising the perfect swing and shot.
- Then start the clear-key – 'Three-hundred-and-fifty-eight million' – and belt the thing.

There's no doubt that this process was very helpful. I certainly seemed to be able to stand over the ball on a tricky hole and not worry so much about where it was going to go.

Carey had developed a practice method called the thirty-two-ball drill, which, for me, was the best part of the process, revolutionising my practice time. You line up thirty-two balls in groups of four. You hit four with full pre-shot routine while thinking about whatever you are currently working on with your swing. The clear-key is not used during this phase. If you are working on keeping your hands high at the top of your back-swing, for example, then this is your thought during the swing for the first four shots. Now hit four balls using the clear-key, repeating the phrase during the swing to block out any thought about the mechanics. Follow this alternating drill through the remaining balls, first hitting four with swing thought, then four with clear-key. Carey refers to this drill as four balls on 'manual' and four balls on 'automatic', automatic being the clear-key shots.

This drill is designed to help you with your swing out on the course. If you don't see a change in your striking ability after the first thirty-two balls, then you perform the drill again. This process injected a tighter structure into my practice and probably halved the number of balls I hit each week.

Spurred on by the encouragement from Mark and Carey, and with just seven weeks to go, I started to play a lot of full rounds in the evening. An effortless 75 out with Stuart and several other rounds in the mid-70s showed that I was really getting back on track. I was filled with confidence again and it seemed to be just a matter of time before my perfect round would come together. But I had failed to notice, or at least pay attention to, a few curious developments that were creeping into my game.

I was consistently playing the first six holes at level par or up to two under. At the 165-yard par-three seventh hole, however, I began to struggle with a mental block. I would stand at the tee and end up worrying excessively about the out-of-bounds area on my left. I'd freeze on the tee box. My problem shot was generally always a slice, so this hole shouldn't have caused me any concern. But here I was, starting to hook balls out of bounds left. If I made it through safely, I would regularly hit the turn at level par. And then the trouble would start. I began to 'blow up' over the last nine holes. Time and time again. What should have been a great round would suddenly turn out a disaster.

It's an annoying psycho-babble word that I hate, and a concept that I used to dismiss, but this definitely seemed to be a classic case of 'self-sabotaging'. I was so near my goal by now that each time I went out I could feel the pressure mounting in case this would be the Big Day. The feeling would ease when I hit a bad shot that would put me past the point of no return, which was, in my mind, about two or three over par. I believed that I would play my par round with a long succession of pars and no double bogeys. Being a few over par, I didn't feel I could save the game with a string of birdies, despite the fact that I'd birdied practically every hole on the course by this stage. This belief meant that the minute the score ticked past a couple over, I would give up. I knew I still had the guts of two months to go, and rather than get the challenge out of the way early I seemed to be subconsciously, or maybe even consciously, striving to take it right up to the wire.

Gradually, these niggles in my game increased and my scoring began to creep back out into the 80s again. I was practising just as hard, if not harder, than ever and my short game in particular was improving enormously. My scoring, however, was getting worse. Debbie was busy with the lesson season again, so I didn't want to bother her too much, and anyway, I was convinced that my problems were purely mental. The clock seemed to be ticking ever louder. I still had my week off work ahead of me but the pendulum was swinging the wrong way at the wrong time.

I seemed to be capable of the most astonishing swings in performance. Generally, my best golf was played out on a nice quiet course in the evening on my own. Ideally, I'd be working on something simple in my swing and not really counting the score. Yet even this idyllic state was letting me down. I shot a 75 out with Stuart and then proceeded to lose five balls in nine holes the next night out playing on my own.

Somewhat stereotypically for an Irishman, I was having problems with alcohol, too. I had a wave of parties around this time and, rather inconveniently, the day after each of these late nights I would inevitably be lined up to play golf. The logical thing, of course, would have been to say to Lesley, 'Don't worry, darling, I'll drive,' and just pass myself with a couple of Coca-Colas. Logic, however, rarely features particularly strongly in my brain and, with the pressure mounting, I found it so much easier to get, as we quaintly say here, blocked at every available opportunity. Most of my friends knew about the challenge, so at each outing I'd be bombarded with questions about how it was going. With progress seemingly halted again, it was easier to answer with a cheeky grin or a confident smile if I'd had a few drinks.

The resulting rounds on the following days were complete disasters and very possibly part of this mystical sabotage process. It became all too easy to write off my chances because I had a hangover. The mind is a mysterious beast and capable of tricking you in all sorts of strange ways.

Once more, the support of my mastermind group helped me enormously at this time. Chris, an alcoholic who had been dry for eleven years, had seen his illness wipe out at least ten years of productive life. Since the start of his recovery, he had become very active in his local Alcoholics Anonymous. He worked regularly with alcoholics who were trying to stop drinking, and had probably heard every excuse in the book. To say that he was firm with me was an understatement. During a phone call he made it crystal clear that if alcohol was causing me any sort of trouble at all, then I did have a problem and should seek out my local AA.

Inside, I sounded an enormous 'Eeeeeeeeeeeeeek!' Outwardly, I replied, in as unshocked a way as possible, 'Bloody hell, Chris. I get what you're saying but it's really not as bad as that. I've just had a few drinks too many on a couple of nights because that has eased the stress.'

'And has that then caused you a problem with your golf?' he continued firmly.

'Well, yes,' I blurted out, a tad indignantly, 'but I'm certainly not an alcoholic.'

'If it causes you a problem with your golf or any other part of your life, then you are effectively having a problem with drink.'

'OK,' I wriggled uncomfortably, 'I understand what you're saying but I don't think you realise the culture here. It's very drink-based, certainly very different from many other parts of the world.'

'John – I grew up in Boston and live in LA. Don't you think I know about alcohol-based cultures?'

'Well, yes, I suppose you do.' It was hard to argue with him.

'Look, what I'm saying is that you have got to understand what alcohol does to you. It is a depressant and, as such, it will have a detrimental effect on your ability to deal with pressure. You have already proved this. Do not drink between now and the end of the challenge. If this thing is truly important to you, then that's what you have to do.'

I was pretty shocked by this conversation, no doubt about it. Clichés aside, there is a strong drinking culture in Ireland and I was as guilty as the next (slightly tipsy) man of accepting that drinking a lot is simply what we do. By pinpointing precisely how my drinking the night before was affecting my performance on the course the next day, Chris made the destructive nature of what I was doing very clear. His argument made complete sense and I paid attention to it.

I did not (and do not) have a drink problem that would necessitate a visit to an AA meeting, but it was a very valuable lesson in just how much we all accept alcohol here as a normal part of social life and how destructive it can be if we lean on it in times of stress. What an infinitely depressing and clichéd situation it would have been if I'd failed the challenge as a result of 'taking to the drink'. I cringed at the thought of people gossiping about me, shaking their heads and saying, 'God, how Irish is that!' So I wised up pretty sharpish and took Chris's advice about giving up the drink until the challenge was over.

I booked a lesson with Debbie and recounted my tales of woe and frustration. I told her that I thought I was striking the ball well and that my problems were all mental. Debbie once more disagreed. Working so much on my own, with such a long time since the last lesson, I'd developed a couple of problems with my swing. I had reverted to the standard hacker's slice swing path of in-to-out, with a lovely big loop at the top of my swing. My posture was wrong (too stooped over) and there wasn't enough hip and shoulder turn. Fairly basic stuff, but it would require a lot of work to get it right. I debated with her as to whether I should be working on such changes at this late stage when I was still scoring relatively well, but she was insistent that the errors were too fundamental to ignore.

Once more I went back to Hogan's *Five Lessons* and dragged out the hundreds of swing videos I'd amassed over the year to try to clarify what it was that I was trying to change. Posture was easy. I just needed to stand more upright. I worked hard in front of the mirror at home and used the mirror behind the driving-range bays to fix this.

Swing path is more difficult. It is such a fundamental error and one that afflicts so many golfers. On a busy night at the range you can walk along the rows of golfers and around eighty per cent of them will be battling with a loop and an in-to-out swing path.

I had read online about a drill – the flashlight drill – that can be beneficial in helping to fix this error and I decided to give it a go. I nipped down to my local hardware store to purchase a couple of small torches. What I found on offer was even better. Flashlights with a laser pointer. I bought two and fixed them to an old five iron, using duct tape – one attached to the butt of the club, pointing at my chest (at address), and one to the shaft of the club just below the grip, pointing downwards.

The theory is that when you swing, the lights trace out the swing path. If you're swinging well, the lights trace one smooth line; if you're swinging badly, they trace something more like a figure of eight and you immediately see where you have gone wrong. Like a lot of changes in golf you must exaggerate the change beyond what feels normal to reach a stage where you have fixed whatever problem you had been having. This drill helps you see exactly how much you need to exaggerate the feeling and is very effective.

Over several nights, after dark, I spent a long time out in the garden swinging the club until the new path looked normal and the lights traced the one smooth path. Anyone viewing my back garden at that time must have wondered what was going on. Little laser lights flashing around like there'd been an alien landing.

Practice was required at the range to groove in the new swing and I used Carey's thirty-two-ball drill to help make the swing permanent. A few of these early range sessions were absolute disasters, with repeated shanking of the ball off into the trees. I was working at the end of the range, where most people don't venture. But a guy who I had played with in the early days spotted me and came down for a chat. The look on his face as he watched me send ball after ball off into the woods was priceless – somewhere between horror and pity. My one venture onto the course during that week was pretty horrific, too; I was six over par after nine holes.

It had set me back about a week. Despite this, I wasn't all that concerned. Range work and hard graft on my swing was my comfort zone, and with Carey's drills I knew that with six weeks left I could still be all right. It just meant more blisters and a few more aches and pains, but I was well used to that by now. It also helped me fuel my Rocky-gearing-up-for-the-big-fight fantasies. In the gym I saw myself pounding the meat carcasses and preparing for my run up the steps of the Philadelphia Museum of Art, with the music building in the background.

All this work on my swing had happened during a period of particularly dreadful weather and I wouldn't have been able to play on the course with any regularity. Indeed, the rain became so bad that the course was shut for a few days and the forecast threatened ten full days of rain ahead. A wave of panic started to rise inside me. More than ever, I worried that planning a May-to-May time-frame had been rash on my part. A week's setback had been just about acceptable at this stage but a further week due to bad weather would land me in deep trouble.

I was sorely tempted to nip off to Spain for a week, but there was simply no way I could afford the time away from work and family. It could have provided me with a perfect opportunity to play without interruption and maybe dispel some of the demons that were hovering around me. My sense of panic was increasing steadily by the day. I thought long and hard about Spain and even chatted to Seve about it in the car. He agreed with me that it would almost certainly help my game, but I'd made my commitment to complete the challenge in a certain way and there was a limit to how much selfishness I could impose on Lesley and the others. I also wasn't convinced that I'd benefit from practising there, no matter how much sunshine there was, as my feelings of guilt would have been through the roof.

On a soaking-wet course I managed to get out and scramble an 81. This included some silly errors and a ball lost because it plugged in the fairway. Ten shots clear of my goal with a month to go. Not good. Not good at all.

By early May I was on the edge of another meltdown and really struggling with the weather and my game. The North was shrouded in a perpetual drizzle, which, although the course was kept open, meant that golf was a pretty unpleasant experience. The 'Black Dog' started to hang over me and I kept making fundamental errors on several holes to sabotage my round. My driving was becoming erratic, too, and I was spraying the ball with no control off the tee.

Once more I was convinced that my problems were psychological, until I spoke to Debbie briefly outside her office one day. I casually swung my club a couple of times in front of her while I discussed my woes. She saw straightaway that I was opening the clubface a fraction at the top of my swing. Back to the range I went and it was an immediate cure. Proof again that I should have spent a little more time squeezing in ten-minute lessons with Debbie. It would have stopped these niggles turning into bigger problems.

My growing obsession with Hogan and his search for perfection wasn't helping my game either. Hogan's life story is hugely compelling to golfers. There are literally dozens of different books about the great man, so for someone with obsessive tendencies like me there were rich pickings. I was spending far too much time reading about him. I also spent too much time watching his swing and attempting to absorb his style into my own swing. My mobile filled up, much to Debbie's exasperation, with lots of short clips of Hogan's swing, which I would proudly show her. But Hogan's swing, and Seve's to a certain extent, was the product of a different era and different technology.

I was buying into the romantic notion that I could model myself on two of the greatest players of all time and succeed. Incredibly, I still felt that if I ignored all other advice and turned myself into a Seve/Hogan clone, it would all work out. I'd stand there at the eleventh hour on the three-hundred-and-sixty-fifth day, with Seve and Hogan hoisting me onto their shoulders. I even imagined that, following their lead, I might spend another year trying to get on tour. Nonsense.

Seve and Hogan had helped me many, many times during the year but there is no doubt that this wasn't one of them. The heightened pressure of the final furlong was making me lose a proper grip on reality and, more importantly, a grasp of the simple swing mechanics that Debbie had so effectively taught me.

The Week Off Work

Keep true to the dreams of thy youth.
FRIEDRICH VON SCHILLER

So here it was. The trumpets sounded and the red carpet was laid out. The greatly anticipated second week of May finally arrived. The week when I was going to 'do it'. A week off work with nothing to do but play golf and wrap the whole thing up. I'd been counting on this week as being The Week for a long time. During the past year, I hadn't taken a full day off work to play golf. I'd always been to work in the morning or later in the day, so a full week off was an incredible treat.

It seemed like a dream and, to a certain extent, it started out that way. The weather had changed for the better and on day one I disappeared to the end of the driving range to the little pitching-and-chipping section with a couple of bottles of water and a PowerBar, raring to go. Much of my recent motivation had sprung from my admiration of the Fijian golfer Vijay Singh. This was primarily due to his powerful work ethic, and also because, at that time, he was number one in the world rankings and a solid four years older than me. Any thoughts of being too old and creaky for the challenge could immediately be dismissed by an image of Singh grafting at the range in the glow of a setting sun. Last man standing and number one in the world.

I spent an hour or so pitching and chipping to my shag bag and then sat down in the sun for a rest. What a great life. It seemed that, even now, in a very small way, the challenge had already changed my life. I may not have been playing golf for a living, but I could glimpse how great that must be. A week spent practising and playing golf, even under immense pressures, appeared to me a much more appealing job than sitting in an office or running cafés, restaurants or garden centres.

I lay back in the warm spring air and enjoyed the luxury of it all. Once more the Walter Mitty part of my brain kicked into gear and a variety of ludicrous notions started to drift through my mind. Singh was forty-two and I was now thirty-eight. What was to stop me taking this thing even further? I had made huge progress in eleven months. What if I were able to devote two or three solid years to improving? I could easily get to scratch in pure handicap terms within another year (or so I naively thought) and then I'd take a couple of strokes off each year after that. I'd soon hit the plus-3 or 4 handicap zone that could get me into the professional ranks.

Or I could concentrate on being an amateur, rationalise my business career and try a shot at the majors as top British amateur. If at forty-two Singh could be the best golfer in the world – even better than the theoretically unbeatable Tiger – then what possible argument was there against me trying to get to top amateur or even journeyman-pro status by the same age? As I lay in the sun it all seemed so plausible. Never mind the fact that I was still four shots off a level-par round.

Seve walked over and nudged me with a sand wedge.

'Hey, Meester Richardson, eet's a great dream, certainly. And eet might even be possible. But today we just need to keep workin' on this goal. So, let's get thees one par round out of the way and then we'll see. OK, Meester Big Shot?'

'Yep, Seve.'

I picked up my club again and got back to work.

That afternoon I went out on the course on my own. The conditions were perfect – I had no distracting partners, no pressure to perform in front of anyone, and it was just the start of the week. Yet despite some excellent golf, I shot an 80. Nothing to get too concerned about but still nine full strokes off my target on the week when it was all supposed to come together. And the round hadn't even been plagued by any 'bad luck' for me to blame it on. I'd even been concerned before I went out that I didn't have a witness if I should achieve my goal. As it was, there'd have been little point in having a witness for a score of 80.

That night I sat down with a sheet of A3 paper and began to map out my weak areas. My driving was very much back on track with Debbie's last little tweak and my long and mid-irons were the same. I was using them so little at Blackwood, of course, that there didn't seem much point in concentrating on them anyway. The focus came back to short game and putting. I had lost a couple of shots in the sand during my round that day, so I decided that I'd put a bit of practice into that. The next afternoon I was due to play with my dad at his course on the far side of Belfast. In many ways it was very similar to the Blackwood challenge and I was confident that I could reel off a decent score.

In the morning I got up early and spent a full two hours in the practice bunker. Another couple of hours on my pitching and chipping and I was brimming with confidence. The result? Another 80. My game was good and my practice in the bunker had paid off so well that I even holed a shot from a horrendously difficult bunker. The basic pattern was the same, though – good golf but some scrappiness that contributed to a few dropped shots. Too much loss of concentration and allowing myself to be put off by too many distractions, such as other golfers on adjoining fairways.

I was two days down and not even breaking 80. I should have been shooting 72s and 73s at this stage and getting cross with myself for a couple of lipped putts – not trying to justify where I was losing eight or nine shots.

Even worse, I had a family outing planned for the next day, so I wouldn't be able to squeeze in a full round. I could feel the panic again welling up inside. Like a kid at the start of the summer holidays, the week had seemed to stretch ahead like an eternity of opportunity when it began. Now that I was reaching the halfway mark and getting nowhere fast, things weren't looking so good. This was definitely not part of my plan.

That night I got out and played the first six holes before the light disappeared. Level par as usual. I decided to rework my distances with my sand wedge and lob wedge in the fading light up to the sixth green. An hour of blissful practice in semi-darkness restored some of my faith in my abilities. I had reached a stage where I had become capable of landing ball after ball with great accuracy to within a few feet of the flag. It felt good, especially when I recollected how much bother I'd had with this tricky green, with its bunkers at the front and the ground falling away steeply at the back.

All my hard work with the wedges had produced great confidence in these distances. But that only served to increase my frustration at my inability to score properly. I had become so confident with these distances that, in my mind's eye, I used to play an instructional video out on the course on the sixth hole, showing fictional golfers how to use the 3x4 system. I would shoot three drives off the tee to slightly different distances and then stroll up talking to the fictional camera about how I would play the next shots. The wedge shots in would roughly equate to 60 to 90 yards. I'd pull out my little distance sheet and then select the club that matched best and hit it. I'd move to the next, still commentating, measure it out and then hit it. Finally, I'd hit the last one, turn to the camera and glibly say: 'Now, that's how you do it. Try it. I think you'll like it.'

The last line is stolen from a Jack Nicklaus video but it went a long way to illustrate just how confident I had become with this method. On more than one occasion with these 'recordings' I'd shoot the ball so close on all three shots that I'd reel off three birdies. Effortless practice, however, and a clear ability to play in a practice environment was not translating onto the course for scoring rounds. More than ever before, I needed to regroup, as it were, and calm down. The strange thing was that my game at every level was better by far than it had been in October when I shot my 78, and yet I didn't seem capable of stringing together a score to beat even that.

That evening my idle ponderings were shattered by the sound of gunshot. In Northern Ireland we theoretically didn't do this type of thing any more. An uneasy peace had descended over the country in the past few years and even in the bad old days we rarely shot people for attempting golf challenges. A couple more shots and I started to get alarmed. I guessed it was the poachers out looking for rabbits, and with my dark clothes and black bag, there was every chance they wouldn't see me. Half terrified and half laughing at the absurdity of it, I quickly scuttled back to the clubhouse, jangling my clubs loudly to alert them to my presence.

I arrived in to see Debbie's car still sitting there. She had heard the shots, too, and laughed when she saw my face.

'You're lucky you didn't end up like a teabag out there,' she said.

There are all manner of hazards to face in golf, but being shot at is rarely one of them.

A couple of days later I was out again with another friend, Nick Cann, to see if I could perform better with a different playing partner. A graphic designer who had recently reinvented himself by becoming a novelist, Nick was very supportive. He was interested in my challenge, in the possibilities it held as a life-changing experience. His own life had changed with the publication of his first book and we talked at great length about what makes people turn their backs on their dreams. And, more to the point, what it is that finally drives others to take action to make their dreams come true.

Nick's great-great-grandfather, J.H. Taylor, belonged to that great triumvirate of golfing masters that also included Harry Vardon and James Braid. Taylor won five British Opens and went on to help set up the PGA. According to Nick, it was his esteemed relation who taught Vardon the famous grip. So the Vardon grip, as it is known today, should rightly be called the 'Taylor grip'.

When Nick and I stepped onto the course, I was enjoying his company and his anecdotes, and my game started off very well. He was impressed by what he saw and I was happy and relaxed.

Too relaxed. And my brain saw this as excuse number 342 not to continue to concentrate and I breezed in with yet another frustratingly careless 80.

To be honest, I was getting *really* desperate. I'd confided to Lesley and John Shortt at *Golf Digest* that I didn't think I'd be able to pull it off. To everyone else, I remained aggressively confident but in my heart of hearts I was starting to lose faith. I wrote in my *Golf Digest* article that month that what I needed was golfer's Viagra. I needed something to help me get it up on the course.

What made my performance even more frustrating was the fact that I managed to shoot the par-three course at level par without even trying. It had happened when I was out attempting to measure as accurately as possible my yardages with each iron. I felt I was guilty of overestimating how far I could hit each club – a failing I shared with practically every other amateur in the land. This meant that on a couple of holes I wasn't even using the correct club since I was looking for a measurement as opposed to getting it right at the pin. After the first nine holes I realised I was one under and by simply concentrating on my shot-making and not worrying about my score, I ended up level par.

So was this the long sought-after level-par round? Nope. There was no witness for a start, and it was on a course that, by any stretch of the imagination, didn't count. My original challenge had been that the round was to be played on the Hamilton course. What this did prove, however, was that my shot-making was excellent and I genuinely was at a level where my dream round was within my grasp. The only difference between the Hamilton course and the par-three course was a lot more tee shots with the driver. With that being generally the strongest part of my game, it seemed that shooting a level-par round on the main course should actually be easier than on the par three.

In other words, it all came back to dealing with those demons in my head. On the main course, there no longer seemed to be any situation that worked for me. Playing with good golfers, bad golfers or even just by myself – they all resulted in the same problem of stresses and sabotage. Hence my need for Viagra, or the golfer's version of it. I was now staring humiliation in the face. It wouldn't have been so bad if I'd given up a few months ago, pleading work pressures or some such excuse. But here I was right at the end, practising like a madman, playing some beautiful golf in all areas and even putting with some success, and yet I couldn't seem to bring it all together.

But I kept at it. Regardless of how I was scoring, I knew that my basic game had reached a new level. The par-three round had proved that. I may have been shooting 80s but, paradoxically, my abilities were streets ahead of where I had been when I'd last been shooting in the 70s. Every single aspect of my shot-making was better. What I wasn't doing was translating that onto the course.

I spoke with Carey and a variety of other experienced golfers and they all told me the same thing – relax and let it happen. Don't keep pushing it. I re-read one of Rotella's books where he talks about periods of great progress followed by long plateaus of no improvement. This all made sense, yet it wasn't doing me any good and I had less than two weeks left to go. I didn't have the time to languish on a long plateau or take a Zen approach to just 'let it happen'.

I needed good, clear advice of the sports-psychology kind. Desperately. Some magic ingredient that would propel me over the finish line like Roger Bannister. I put myself in a what-would-Tiger-do? scenario. Tiger is the ultimate exponent of someone who just keeps at it. Every aspect of his game – his course management, his physical shape, his diet, his practice routines, even his rest periods – are all outstanding. And when something isn't quite right, he is prepared to keep digging to change it. He does whatever it takes to help him towards his dream: beating Nicklaus's record wins in the majors.

But it's hard to keep thinking like Tiger and I started to look for other ways out of the dilemma. I found myself trying to rewrite the challenge title in some sort of catchy way that wouldn't look like a cop out, like 'From Scratch to Scratch in Eighteen Months' or 'From Scratch to Scratch in Two Summers', but all my efforts reeked of compromise and failure.

The dream had begun to fade, to look impossible, and I was slowly giving up. I was allowing myself to believe that I should have allocated eighteen months to the challenge rather than one year. Therefore, there was no need to be so hard on myself. 'Just relax, Johnnie Boy – you've worked hard and you'll get there eventually.' That particular variety of inner voice is the one I hate the most. He sits smugly in your head with a comforting smile and superficially tries to help. Most of the time I can manage to boot him out of my life but when you're feeling vulnerable his charms can easily get to you. He stands there beckoning towards the comfy chair with a glass of burgundy in one hand and the TV remote in the other. When you're tired and full of self-doubt, he has the power to brush aside his opponent – that feisty wee inner voice that says, 'Get off your ass. Don't quit.' It's the smug, wheedling voice that holds out the false promise of making things easy and offers the pale reward that comes with instant gratification of the shallow kind. And it's pure BS, but we all listen to this voice at one time or another. Some people never manage to listen to anything else.

What was worse was that even before the year was over I received my first 'I told you that you couldn't do it at the beginning and I was right' post from someone on the forum. I can't stand 'I told you so' people and the Internet provides the perfect place for them to flourish. I lost it when I was replying and most of my posts were moderated by the forum controller. I decided to stop contributing to the forum until the challenge was over.

Instead of listening to all this negative stuff, I needed to be doing a full 'Michael Schumacher' with the challenge. The German, seven-time world-champion Formula One driver had an astonishing ability to keep trying right to the very end of every race. Even when he had seemingly lost all chance of a win he continued to drive at a relentless pace. Time and again this allowed him to pick up championship points and even the odd win, when a few drivers had dropped out ahead. It's a mindset I deeply respect but it's not one that I can always summon up. When I see failure staring me in the face, I find it too easy to listen to that smug little voice telling me to ease off. The true measure of a great sportsman is the ability to ignore those voices and keep at it long after hope has gone.

I would force myself to sit down with Seve, Hogan, Senna, Tiger and other folk like Donald Trump, and get them to help me fight off the lethargy and doubt. Everytime I felt like ducking out of practice or found myself wishing the whole thing was over, I'd get them to hurl abuse at me to fire me up. This would keep me going for another few days.

What also helped at this stage was an article I read in one of the golf magazines about a guy called Bob MacDermott who had lost a leg and an arm in a horrendous combine-harvester accident. Miraculously, he had recovered and now, thanks to a specially designed false arm and leg, he held his club course record of 66. This guy looked out from the page with a face and an expression reminiscent of John Wayne. Now *there* was somebody with true grit. I bet he didn't have teams of fictional heroes booting him up the ass every day to keep him going. I bet he didn't sit at home trying not to drink away his sorrows or bleating on about golfer's Viagra.

The article struck a chord with me, and out of that man's courage, I found a smidgen of my own true grit. His story wasn't just inspiring – it made my challenge look pathetic in comparison. Here was a guy with one leg and one arm who was beating everyone else at his club. And here I was, struggling to break par with no bigger disability than a sore wrist and slightly dodgy hips! What the hell was that all about?

It was a hugely motivating moment. But lacking a full set of John Wayne genes meant that the inspiration I got from this story only took me so far. My passion and drive continued to ebb away, and my anger at the folk who were saying 'I told you so' stopped translating into proper 'I'll show the bastards' results.

I knew for certain this time that the problem with my golf was in my head. You simply couldn't argue with my ability to play at the range. As a last-ditch attempt, I scoured the Internet looking for a golf-specific hypnosis course. I'm a great believer in the power of hypnosis, having used it previously for a sleeping problem. Why I hadn't thought of it earlier? In a flurry of activity I bought three sets of hypnosis tapes and even paid way over the odds in a macho-bidding episode on eBay for a Paul McKenna tape.

I listened to them all several times over and the message was effectively the same. Keep calm, trust your swing and let it happen. What Carey and the others had advised, in fact. It didn't work. It didn't make any difference at all. Perhaps I didn't give it long enough but, then, I didn't have the time to spend relaxing, listening to tapes and getting into a trance only to get nowhere when I went back onto the course. I might as well have been listening to Celine Dion. And my irritation with the let-it-happen concept was reaching a similar level to that which I would have felt if I had been listening to the lovely Ms Dion. So I ditched the hypnosis and abandoned a bit more of my hope along with it.

With one week to go, I had nothing more to show than another couple of 80s. I kept practising and kept playing but it just wasn't coming together, and with every round I finished, I had less and less confidence that I might do it. It was incredibly frustrating.

I was getting tired, too. Truly deep-down tired. Tired of the constant practice and play, tired of the relentless reading and video-watching, and tired of pissing off my business partners and my family. Tired of it all.

The Final Stretch

Now, I say to you today, my friends, even though
we face the difficulties of today and tomorrow, I
still have a dream.

MARTIN LUTHER KING, JR

It was at this low point that I read an e-mail from my Belgian
friend, Annick, telling me about a performance coach. David
Walters had been working very successfully with some golfers in
the north of England, using a technique called 'tapping'. This
experience made him exactly the type of person I had been
searching for, but his method seemed odd and I have to admit I
was less than enthusiastic. But Annick had worked very hard to
help me and it would have been extraordinarily rude of me to
refuse to give it a go.

I contacted David by e-mail and provided him with a few
details outlining my specific problems. We had six days to go
and David very generously said he was happy to spend an hour
and a half with me on the phone every day until we completed
the task. On the one hand, this horrified me – the thought of
having to spend that amount of time on the phone and still play
and practise seemed like one obsessional nightmare too many.
On the other hand, I was intrigued by the calm, optimistic tone
of his e-mail and the matter-of-fact way he believed he could
solve my problems. He was either very naive, I thought, or
genuinely did have something new to offer.

Even if it didn't work, I told myself, I'd still be able to look myself in the face and say I kept fighting to the very end. I'd be able to feel that I had done a Tiger with the challenge. Even if I failed, I could say with hand on heart that I never gave up.

David sent me some details about the technique, along with a small questionnaire to fill out, which I dutifully returned. Although I didn't understand his approach, it seemed to have been very effective in situations not dissimilar to mine, and he certainly had some impressive testimonials from other golfers. I wasn't confident by any means but my tiny flickering flame of hope was burning ever so slightly brighter.

At nine on the evening of Saturday 19 May, I left Lesley to enjoy the DVD we had rented and trudged wearily down to Aimee's play room to phone David. Feeling apprehensive, and breaking my self-imposed drinking ban, I brought a glass of wine with me for moral support.

David explained that he wanted to use a technique called EFT: emotional freedom technique. EFT, he said, was similar to acupuncture, though it didn't use needles. Instead, the various energy, or meridian, points were stimulated by 'tapping' them to release any negative emotions. I had long been convinced of the value of acupuncture, so this wasn't that hard a sell for me. Then David suggested that I ask Lesley to come in and tap along, too, since her energy would help me. This was a tad too 'Californian' for my liking and I could well imagine Lesley's face if I asked her to interrupt her evening to come and 'tap' her meridian points. I felt that there was, in fact, a good chance that she would tap me quite hard with one of the weighted clubs that were littering the house.

Trying not to sound too negative, I politely informed David that I didn't think inviting Lesley would be a good idea and that I'd prefer to do it alone. He was happy with this and proceeded to explain in a little more detail what these points were and how the process worked. There is a variety of methods, but basically it involves tapping a sequence of points on the face and upper body while repeating a phrase that articulates your problem. It had been extremely effective in clearing phobias, such as fear of flying or the fear of spiders, he said. It had also been used with great success for Vietnam vets to clear long-term traumatic memories and had helped other sufferers of post-traumatic stress disorder. You focus on your fear or the incident that caused the fear and then tap the points to break down this negative flow of emotions.

Still sceptical, but reassured by the fact that David didn't sound like a complete nutter and was starting to talk in a very insightful way about my problems, I began to change my mind a little. David asked me a lot of probing questions about my motivation for the challenge and some very specific problems I was experiencing on the course. My biggest and most obvious mental block still revolved around the seventh tee – the par-three hole that had been causing me problems for the past few months.

On a recent occasion out playing with Stuart, I'd arrived at the seventh tee one under par and lost three balls in a row into the woods. My fear of the hole had reached epic proportions. It was preposterous. I then spent an hour out on the tee late one evening with my three wood, perfecting a chip shot that would take me the 165 yards to the green. It's not the worst technique in the world to use to break a pattern on a hole, and in a vague, sticking-plaster sort of way it worked. As long as you can get a few good shots away on the 'horror hole', then you tend to break the association of whacking it into the trees or lake or whatever.

In my case, though, I'd been building up this problem all year and when I went back to my normal six or seven iron, it would just rear its head again. So a sticking plaster is all that it was. It wasn't going to cure the problem. I desperately needed to solve the underlying issue, whatever that might be.

David asked me to imagine that I was on the tee and then asked me to rate the intensity of my fear or concern on a scale of one to ten – one being no fear at all and ten being all-out panic. Even thinking about standing there had my heart beating faster and the thought of standing over the ball with my seven iron in hand was a full ten on the stressometer. He made me focus on this image and repeat the phrase 'concern over seventh tee' while I tapped on the meridian points on my face and neck.

When we had finished the round of tapping, he made me imagine the tee again and attribute a number to it. Bizarrely, the level of distress I felt was much lower than before. I experienced a very odd sensation, and a freeing up of my shoulders. I still felt some concern, so I rated it six and we tapped again for the same issue. This time I felt that three more accurately reflected my level of concern. This seemed miraculous. My scepticism was rapidly disappearing. One more round of tapping and, amazingly, I was down to zero. I could clearly imagine myself at the seventh tee, bent over the ball, and had no sense of worry whatsoever. It was an incredible feeling. The whole thing was surreal. If I needed proof that the tapping technique worked, then this was plenty. My glass of wine sat there with an initial gulp taken from it and I suddenly had no need for any more. This was genuinely fascinating.

Now we moved on to some more specifics. He wanted to deal with similar problems before we tackled any of the bigger issues in relation to the challenge itself. A classic fear of this type for golfers is the shot on the first tee. Particularly if there is an audience around. Thankfully, this was a problem I didn't have, but I did have a major fear of playing shots from adjoining fairways with people waiting. When my ball would drift onto another fairway and people would have to wait for me to play, I'd panic. I've managed to lose many a ball by quickly hacking away in an effort to get out of the other players' way, even in the middle of a round I'd been playing well.

David first applied a bit of common-sense thinking to the situation by asking how I felt when somebody was playing on my fairway. Within reason, I've no issue with it and don't mind if the player goes through a full pre-shot routine to hit a decent shot. David then asked how long my routine would take in the same situation. And I realised, of course, that my full routine would only take about ten seconds longer – so little time to have to wait in the course of a four-hour round, in fact, that no one would bother about it at all.

We then imagined I was standing on an adjoining fairway with people waiting for me on the tee. Once more I could feel the panic welling up inside. And once more a few rounds of tapping meant that the issue had been totally dispelled. I could imagine calmly walking to the ball, waving to the folk on the tee, and going through my full pre-shot routine without any sense of anxiety.

Next, we dug a little deeper into some of the issues concerning my motivation and general feelings of not being able to pull it off. We talked at length about Sam Torrance and his 'dream on' comment. It had been such a strong motivator for so long and yet it had now turned into an 'excuse' for me to walk away from the challenge. After some work, David helped me to understand the fact that, for all Sam Torrance's incredible successes as a golfer, he didn't know anything about me or my level of ability, and he had never attempted to do what I was proposing.

When I started out on the challenge, it seemed an easy matter to stick a metaphorical two fingers up to the doubters, but now that I fully grasped how difficult it was, it had become just as easy to agree with them. It occurred to me that, in an odd way, the golfer's mindset that I had been so strongly critical of had gradually made its way into my own thinking. The better I had become, the more I thought like a golfer, and the harder it was for me to ignore these 'truths' and keep thinking rationally about the game. With David's help, I clearly saw how and why my thinking had altered.

He then told me something I already knew. That I was playing all parts of my game better than I had when I shot my 75, and my short game, in particular, was in a different league. We tapped for these issues and then turned to how I felt about the big round itself. When I began the challenge, I clearly remember thinking that as long as I could get to a stage where I had birdied half the holes on the course, then it would be a simple process to string a round together at par or less. To an experienced golfer, which was now more or less what I had become, that is a laughable statement, but to an outsider it still rings true. We established that I had now birdied all but three holes on the course and therefore on a purely physical level the goal was well within my grasp. I just needed to get back that level of belief. I had spent much of the year believing that my par round would involve a couple of birdies, a couple of bogeys and the rest pars, and that if I went more than three over par that it was off. I didn't believe I had the game to string together a run of birdies to pull myself back. So, every time I hit three over, I mentally gave up.

We tapped for these fears and concerns and once again I felt a weight being taken off my shoulders. I didn't feel I'd be able to go out and birdie every hole in one go, but I now believed that I had a game good enough to have a string of birdies and pull it back, even if I did have a couple of bad holes.

This very quickly and logically led on to the self-sabotage issue. It became apparent to David as I talked that I found the stress of the back nine very difficult to handle. He made me see that it was actually less stressful for me to have a few bad holes on the back nine and give up than it was to face down the pressure and stick it out. This insight finally brought it home to me that when I was playing, subconsciously I was allowing myself to make errors to ruin the round. Once more we tapped on general feelings of stress and pressure on the back nine and I could feel my concern begin to drift away.

We kept going and worked through a few more specifics, like my fear of 6-foot putts and a regular block I was having with the par-three sixteenth hole, when I suddenly realised it was half past midnight. All my tiredness had evaporated, my wine glass remained practically full and my level of confidence about the challenge was through the roof. My inner 'Schumacher' was as strong as ever and I could only hold contempt for the it's-so-hard John that had been whining away only a few hours previously. I was due to play a round with Stuart the next day and I went to bed believing that I was in with an excellent chance of pulling it off.

It was a relatively pleasant day and we set off in good spirits. The first six holes presented me, as usual, with little difficulty. The big test, of course, was the seventh tee. It was now that I fully realised just how effective David's technique had been. I simply stood there and stroked the ball towards the green. It went arrow-straight at the flag, bounced once and trickled just off the back of the green. I was stunned and so was Stuart. He had witnessed some painful meltdowns on the seventh, and cynical as he was about my episode with David the previous night, he had to acknowledge just what a change this was.

When I got to the ball, it was in a horrible lie and from where I was standing I couldn't see the hole, but I remained full of confidence. I knew my short-game ability had come on in leaps and bounds and David's work with me had reinforced my belief in this. I casually remarked to Stuart, 'I think I can get this in.' He saw my lie and just laughed. This was a pure Ballesteros moment and I truly was Seve for an instant. I imagined him dressed in black, delicately picking the ball out and holing it, and I took a couple of swings and pulled the trigger. The ball flew up high and soft and gently struck the base of the flag. It teetered on the edge of the hole but refused to fall in. Not that I cared. It was another amazing example of the transformation that David had made in my mental approach to the game.

At the end of the first nine holes I looked at my card. A few scrappy holes hadn't helped my case and I sat at one over par. Interestingly, however, I had scored three birdies in nine holes. I had been held back by the thought that I didn't have a game good enough to have more than three birdies in eighteen holes and here I was with three in nine. I didn't even care too much about the score; at this stage, all I was thinking about was the enormous progress I had made with my mental state – all with David's help.

Stuart was having an off day. His golf, a bit like my own, seems to have lots of highs and lows. His game had noticeably improved in the previous few months but this was a true horror day, and by the thirteenth hole he was ready to go home. Still sitting at one over, I was enormously confident about my game, so he stayed on to act as a witness just in case this would be The Day.

Unfortunately, this is where the wheels came off for me. The thirteenth is a tough hole, with trouble on both sides and all around the green. It had ruined a few rounds in the past, so I was a little wary. I sliced my tee shot into the woods never to be seen again and then hooked my next onto the adjoining fairway. Too much bravado with my next shot ended up with me carding an eight for the hole and, for that day at least, the game was off.

But, boy, was I back on track. My mindset had been transformed and the challenge now seemed more possible than ever. A few issues had continued to disturb me, however, and I hoped to resolve them with David later that night. With only four full days to go, the deadline was now incredibly tight, but any thoughts of extending it to an eighteen-month challenge were banished. Four days were four full days of opportunity and I was going to make damn sure I wasn't going to waste them.

That evening I spent another two hours on the phone with David. Needless to say, he was delighted with my progress. We dealt with the issue of the thirteenth hole fairly swiftly and then worked on how I should create a mental bubble around myself when other people are struggling and intruding on my confidence. When I felt any sense of pressure or negative impact from other players or surroundings, I was to pull an imaginary bubble over my head and imagine my surroundings drifting away. This way I would avoid any distraction and fully concentrate on my golf.

We ploughed on, not giving up on the back nine in case there was any residual problem lurking there. By eleven o'clock we were all through, and David wished me luck for the next day. I came off the phone tired, but vaguely wishing we had more issues to deal with. The process is so fascinating, it's almost addictive. It felt very odd to be rid of all my mental problems – almost as if I had used my 'it's all in the mind' argument for so long that I needed it as a prop. I felt strangely naked with nothing to worry about or focus on.

Lobster and Champagne

It's kind of fun to do the impossible.

WALT DISNEY

Stuart was busy, and with his game and mental state in tatters, I didn't want to force him out again anyway. I phoned Richard Gibson, the general manager of the golf centre, and asked if he would go out with me. The last thing I wanted at this stage was to shoot my perfect round and have to arrive in at the clubhouse shouting 'I did it!' to a sea of doubting faces. Richard was keen to help. More heavily involved with the business side of golf than he is as a player, he decided not to play but just walk round the course with me and act as witness.

The great thing about having him along was his attitude. Richard is the most can-do sort of person I know. Having sailed competitively round the world twice, he has absolutely no time for people who say things aren't possible. He is that rare breed who just *does*, without going on about how hard it is. I had talked to him a few times during the year about the project and his attitude had always been very positive. Struggling with a couple of issues at one point, I'd told him I was concerned about my progress. He calmly turned to me and said: 'I don't see what the problem is. You seem to have worked enormously hard, you've made incredible progress, so I've no doubt you'll do it. I really don't see what you have to worry about.'

It wasn't so much what he said, but the way he said it. His

172

voice was full of admiration and encouragement. Not one of your 'Oh come on!' motivational speeches, just a simple statement of the facts as he saw them. He regarded my success almost as a done deed. No one else had spoken to me in quite the same way throughout the entire year. He was a perfect partner for the day.

It rained heavily all morning and the course was closed, causing me a great deal of concern. Here I was all fired up and ready to go but with no course to play on.

The rain stopped at lunch, the sun came out, and we were first on the course. A beautiful, empty parkland course in late spring with raindrops still glistening on the trees is a particularly joyous place to be. I had a wonderful sense of calm as we set off, without a soul about to disturb the silence.

The first six holes were the usual breeze. I parred the first and then birdied the par-five second. Another par at the tricky 210-yard par three helped my momentum and I parred the next two holes. On the 330-yard sixth I hit almost the best drive of my life and was practically on the green. A pitch and a putt meant that I stood on the worrisome seventh tee at two under – my best score yet. It all seemed effortless.

Richard and I talked about all manner of things, mostly unrelated to golf. We had worked on a variety of projects together in the past and chatted about restaurants and the food business in general. He pointed out a few of the rarest trees dotted around the course and spoke about some of his business plans. It all helped me look at the course from a different perspective.

As I stood on the seventh tee I felt no concerns. A slightly scrappy tee shot meant that I dropped a shot here, but I was still one under and my main horror hole was over. The next hole, however, had also caused me some problems in the past. It is a dog-leg left of about 380 yards, with out-of-bounds all down the left-hand side. Recently, though, it had been problem-free and I hadn't mentioned it in my sessions with David, But today, as I stood on the tee, I could feel my fear welling up. There is a little stream at about the 300-yard mark, where a big drive can end up if you're not careful. The safe shot is a three wood but there is also the risk of the ball plugging in a very wet area to the right of the fairway at about this distance. All this started to run through my mind and I found myself freezing over the ball.

The logical thing to do was to walk away and go through the routine again. Instead, I pushed my luck, pulled my ball across to the left and straight into the out-of-bounds. It was on the edge of being a perfect, brave shot over the corner, but a clatter from the trees indicated that my luck had indeed been pushed a fraction too far.

This was a potential turning point. David's words about stringing together birdies and pulling back from these situations echoed in my mind and I calmly reloaded and sent one straight down the middle. A near perfect wedge and a single putt turned a near disaster into a bogey, and I was back to level par.

I parred the par-five ninth and stood on the tenth tee with a reasonable sense of calm. I had been through my two main problem holes and now I just needed to keep it together through the tough back nine. A decent drive to the rough on the edge of the fairway started me on my way, but when we arrived at where the ball should have been there was no sign of it. I could sense panic starting to rise. It had clearly plugged and after a thorough search of five to ten minutes, I accepted that it was gone.

I picked another ball out of the bag and walked slowly back up to the tee. Richard stayed at the bottom of the hill to watch, in case it happened again. This gave me a very useful chance to be alone. The panic was rising now at an uncontrollable rate, blasting my new-found confidence. As I started the walk I was distraught. David's tapping seemed to me mere mumbo-jumbo once more. How on earth had I expected it to work? I couldn't see how I would pull it back over the next nine holes. I had got away with a simple bogey on the eighth and I still had a number of tough holes ahead of me. The tenth is a particularly difficult hole and it looked like a certain six on my card. That would involve not just pars but at least two more birdies on the back nine and there was only one hole where I could reasonably expect to guarantee a birdie.

Halfway up the hill, I began to pull myself together. I started to tap on the acupressure points, which David had indicated were relevant for these issues. I applied some good, old-fashioned logical thinking, too, and committed to at least giving it my best shot. I got to the tee and fumbled an OK drive down the middle. I discreetly tapped again on my way down the hill and tried to talk myself up and out of any residual panic.

There was no miracle recovery this time and a six on my card put me two over, but I felt a vague sense of calmness begin to return. I was experiencing a little anxiety with the thirteenth looming, where I had messed up the day before, but overall I was still in relatively good shape. Normally, I would have given up at this stage and just gone for a decent round in the 70s, but not today. I only had four chances left and that mindset had to go.

The big turning point happened on the next hole. I birdied it and my whole attitude changed back to one of positive expectation. I had pulled back a shot and proved to myself again that I had the birdies within my game. There was also a great birdie opportunity ahead of me at the fourteenth and I just needed to keep it together on the other holes. This was an absolutely crucial moment for me. I slowly moved from having to force myself to *think* it was possible, to achieving a deep level of belief that it was possible. I avoided talk about my score and Richard and I continued to chat about anything other than golf.

I parred the par-three twelfth and stood on the tee at the thir-teenth one over par – just like I had the previous day. If ever there was a shot that I needed to keep straight, then this was it. David had worked his magic on this hole and it was with a huge sense of relief that I hit my drive straight and true down the middle of the fairway. A four iron onto the green and two putts and I was on my way.

The next hole was the big birdie opportunity. A 490-yard par five, the fourteenth is easily reachable in two, as long as the wind isn't blowing. There wasn't a whisper of a breeze all day and I sent my second shot to within 8 feet of the flag.

Richard stopped in his tracks and turned to me. 'John,' he said, 'I haven't seen somebody hit a shot like that, with a swing like that, since I played a round with Tony all those years ago. That was just beautiful.'

This was a huge compliment. Richard was talking about Tony White – the golf pro with whom I had dreamt up the concept of the challenge more than ten years ago. Great friends, he and Richard had been heavily involved in the final design of the course. Now here I was right at the very end of it and with the possibility of success in sight.

I hovered over the putt and realised that if I were to sink it, I'd not only have had my first eagle ever, but I'd be back to one under par, which would be an amazing turnaround in so few holes. A slightly nervous stab left the ball just on the edge of the hole, however, and I tapped in for a birdie four. I was back to level par and beside myself with confidence.

The next hole is a tricky par four with a lake in front of the green. It's my favourite hole on the course, though, and had never caused me any trouble. A huge drive just short of the lake left a pitch on and maybe even another birdie opportunity. But, as I stood over the ball, the water suddenly seemed to loom large in front of me. I stepped back and went through the routine again and then struck the ball. I had badly thinned it and it shot inches above the surface of the water and caught the bank on the other side, before shooting up in the air and zooming across the back of the green. A simple chip and a putt saved par for me. Lucky boy. I could feel the nerves building up, though, and needed to keep on top of it.

Only three holes left and I was desperate for it to be over. The sixteenth hole is a tough par three, with gorse bushes all along the right and a steep drop off to the left into water. It is known as a bit of a card wrecker within the club, and this image was hard to keep out of my mind as I teed up. Mindful of my previous ribbed chip and aware that my nerves were getting to me, I struggled to keep it together on the tee. Richard continued to chat away, talking enthusiastically about a new restaurant in Belfast that had been trading extremely well, but I knew he was just trying to keep my mind off the pressure.

Another swipe at the ball and another thinned shot. The ball never rose more than 3 feet in the air and yet it scuttled the entire distance of the hole right up to the green. If ever the golfing gods had given me a break, then this was it – and their timing was perfect. I looked up to see Hogan, Seve, Palmer, Nicklaus and Jones all standing at the gorse bushes smiling. With a truly appalling shot, I had managed to pull off another par and I only had two relatively simple par fours to go. Hogan tipped his cap to me.

The seventeenth hole has never caused me problems, although it can be tricky, with trouble on both sides. But the trouble on the right isn't an issue for a big driver, and I had always been lucky with the trouble on the left. So I stood on the tee without too much fear. At level par with two to go, I just needed to remain steady and hold it together. This was uncharted territory for me and yet, amazingly, I felt remarkably calm. David and I had dealt with the issue of my notion of 'worthiness' to shoot a level-par round, and as I stood on the elevated tee looking out over the course I genuinely did feel worthy. I *had* worked enormously hard and, finally, I truly believed that I deserved to do it.

As coolly as possible, I stroked my drive down the centre of the fairway and hit a beautiful wedge to within 6 feet of the hole. This time the putt went in and I went berserk. I was going to play the last hole one under par – there was no way I could mess that up. When Stuart and I were out together, we always played the eighteenth hole as a macho, longest drive competition because there is so much fairway to play with. It is almost impossible to lose a ball here and even if I played it badly, I felt I'd be bound to scrape a bogey. I could almost feel tears welling up inside me as all the frustrations of the previous few months came rushing back. I started blabbering to Richard like a madman.

'Oh my God. I can't believe I'm really here. There's no way I won't make it now. This hole is simple. I didn't admit it to you before, but a few weeks ago I didn't think I'd make it. I'd really started to believe all that it's-not-possible bollocks. Can you credit that?'

'John – would you just shut up and finish it off so we can get in and have a drink.'

'Aye, fair comment.'

My drive was straight and true and I proceeded to strike the best second shot I have ever played at that hole. The view of the green is restricted on the second shot, so you're never quite sure whether you have had a good result or not, but when I reached the top of the hill the ball was sitting 7 feet from the pin. Richard laughed and remarked that I didn't seem to be able to put a foot wrong and that's exactly how it had felt for the previous eight holes. It had just flowed perfectly. Even my two poor shots had worked out fine and here I was standing over a putt for a 69 – two full shots below par.

But a round in the 60s seemed surreal. I had been working with David to ensure that I felt worthy of playing in the 70s and shooting level par or better, but playing in the 60s was way out of my comfort zone. It seemed like a stage too far. Golfers on television and on tour shoot rounds in the 60s. Not wee Johnnie Boy from Bangor. It seemed like I was taking too much advantage of the golfing gods' generosity.

I took a stab at the ball but left it a full foot short. So I missed my round in the 60s but a simple tap in meant a solid 70. One under par and 361 days after the start of the challenge.

My jubilation at the previous hole had turned into quiet contemplation and at this stage Richard was more excited than me.

'Lobster and champagne, I think!' he laughed. 'Phone Lesley and I'll book a table.'

Classic Richard. Champagne and lobster. Who was I to argue?

Slightly dazed, I walked over to the office, and with a huge sense of relief, I phoned Lesley.

'Lesley, I did it.'

'Did what?'

'My par round.'

'What? You did it! Really?' And she began to whoop and yell in utter delight.

'Yes I did. I shot a 70 – one under par.'

'Yee-hah!' she shouted.

A little voice piped up in the background.

'What, Mum? What's wrong, Mum? Mum?' It was Aimee, wondering if her poor mother had finally been pushed over the edge.

'Dad did it,' I heard Lesley say. 'He did his golf thing. You know, the round that he's been trying to get all year?'

First a silence. Then, 'Ah, right then, Ted,' – Aimee's favourite expression at that time and a sure sign that I'd let her watch more episodes of *Father Ted* than were strictly healthy for a seven-year-old.

'So we'll not be eating at home tonight,' I told Lesley. 'Get Aimee's homework finished because we're all going out for some lobster!'

'Oh yes we are – you can bet on that!' Lesley laughed.

David was the person I rang next. He was beside himself with delight. There is no doubt that I owed him a huge debt of gratitude. It simply wouldn't have happened without him at that crucial time. Debbie and Stuart were equally delighted.

Richard was waiting at the car park. I thanked him and we arranged to meet later.

Then I climbed into my car, still slightly shell-shocked, and sat quietly for a while. I turned round to see Seve beside me, and Hogan in the back leaning forward with his arms on the back of the seat. He smiled and tipped the edge of his immaculate white cap. In his Texan accent he said: 'You played well. That was a good round of golf. You've worked hard.'

Seve beamed broadly. 'Well, Meester Richardson, wha' abou' tha', my friend? You deserved eet, you know. You worked hard and played great golf. What are you gonna say to all those people now, eh?'

Epilogue
What Was it All About?

If you can dream it, you can do it.
WALT DISNEY

With a sore head, but well fed on lobster and champagne, I sat down the next day with a metaphorical cigar to ponder what it was all about. It felt odd to be back to some sort of normality and not feel guilty when I was doing something unrelated to golf. The challenge had utterly dominated my life over the past year but I knew that it had been an extremely positive process. Certainly painful at times, with periods of frustration and guilt, but never less than completely engrossing all the same. It now seemed to me akin to childbirth. I had my beautiful baby in front of me and I quickly forgot about all the pain it took to get him here.

I felt so grateful to the 'midwives' who had helped me along the way. Debbie, involved from the very beginning, had devoted a great deal of time and effort to the project. It certainly wouldn't have been possible without her. Nor would it have been possible without wisdom and expertise of Jim McLellan and Carey Mumford. And the principles and techniques that David Walters taught me at so crucial a moment will stay with me for the rest of my life. Even Lesley lost her initial scepticism about EFT and became a firm believer when we used the technique (just five minutes' tapping did the trick) to cure her migraines, which has saved her countless days of suffering.

I had lots of support from many friends, but, in particular, I doubt that I could have completed the challenge without Stuart's support. Having him with me on the journey made it all vastly more fun, and I will always be indebted to him for that. A result of the intense competition between us was that Stuart's game came on in leaps and bounds. He went on to win both his club championships and was named player of the year. My mastermind group and a couple of other close friends were also a great support during some of my more self-indulgent, head-in-hands moments.

And, of course, I also have to thank Seve Ballesteros and Ben Hogan. The Seve thing was complex, being so strongly linked back to that wee fella who watched him at the Irish Open more than twenty years before. Part of me will always be fifteen when I see him. He helps me still, every time I play around the green. Whether I'm chipping or pitching, I'll always imagine I'm Seve.

Hogan's influence was different. For golfers throughout the world, he remains an utterly fascinating character. His relentless quest for perfection was inspirational, and the fact that he had probably less innate talent than Seve encouraged me to believe that I, too, could become a good player, good enough to win the challenge. He worked so long and hard for his initial success and spent years barely scraping a living on the tour. And just when he had finally made it, he was involved in a horrific car crash. The story of his slow climb back to success after the accident is an inspiration for golfers the world over. Any time I flagged, I would imagine him telling me to keep at it, 'keep digging dirt', and I'd get there.

At the start of the challenge I proclaimed that I needed to complete the year with my marriage and my job intact. I was very strict about ensuring that I didn't steal too much time away from Aimee, but there is no doubt that it was tough for Lesley, spending night after night alone at home, watching countless episodes of *The West Wing*, while I thrashed away indulgently at the range. But she was immensely supportive throughout, and it simply wouldn't have been possible without her patience and love. A few days after I'd finished, we talked about how tough it had been, and she admitted that it had been much worse for her than she'd ever let on. She told me that she'd felt very lonely and those words hit me tremendously hard. But she knew it was something that I had to do and she was, without a shadow of a doubt, more pleased than anyone else that I had succeeded.

My challenge experience impacted rather differently on my career. By the time it was over, I had already decided to leave the business and was due to start afresh in July. I knew deep down that it was the correct decision. My fellow directors had been very supportive and I wished them every success with the business and said goodbye to the great people who work there.

So I was free to move on. But not to move on and play golf professionally. I loved the challenge, but the life of a professional golfer wasn't for me. I just didn't have the drive or desire to make a career out of it.

My desire to keep improving my golf almost instantly disappeared, too. This is partly the result of sheer overload but also partly because of the way I'd had to motivate myself in the latter phases of the challenge. My primary motivator in the last few months was a moving-away-from-humiliation goal and when I completed the challenge the drive to keep getting better was gone. If I'd focused purely on the joy of the perfect round, I'd probably have been keener to keep improving. Whatever the reason, what I needed now was to take the summer off and spend a lot more time at home with my family. Golf, challenge or no challenge, is still a very time-consuming pastime.

What would I do differently? Very little. The challenge was what it was and it had to be that way. There was no manual to follow because nobody had attempted it before. Therefore the various mistakes I made along the way had to happen. If you don't make the mistakes you can't learn. I used to exasperate Debbie with some of the new theories and principles that I'd found in the latest book or video but if I'd just stuck to a simple lesson-and-practice/play format, I'd never have made it. I needed to do a lot of work on my mental game to help me through all the extra pressure.

With hindsight, though, there was no need to hit thirty-five thousand balls. My practice routine was very loose in the early days and I can now accomplish far more with a hundred balls than I was doing with three hundred balls when I started out. I developed a huge range of practice techniques to help make the process much faster and easier by collating data from many different sources. As the year progressed I became more and more efficient. I sometimes wonder whether, in hindsight, I couldn't have undertaken the challenge in half the time. I'll never know and, anyway, discovering the processes was half the fun.

So just how good a golfer am I now? Well, I'm certainly not a scratch handicapper. It would take at least another year to get to that level with at least as much hard work. I'm what you might call a 'fragile' golfer. Immediately after my big round, I played in a large corporate competition on a very tough course in Belfast. It was wet and windy and I didn't even get close to breaking 80, let alone approach breaking par again. This was a salutary lesson and showed how much my game was based around perfect conditions at Blackwood. It highlighted how I had created a slightly 'plastic' game that wasn't entirely transferable to a range of different courses.

Having said that, I'm a vastly better golfer than I would have been after a year of traditional practice or even a few years of standard golfing improvement. When I think back to the first round in May 2004 and the eights and tens on my card, it seems like a million miles away. A bad day's golf for me now is one where I spray a few drives or have a string of holes where I can't make par. It's still a tough game and still hugely frustrating, but it's a lot more enjoyable than it was when I was shooting in the hundreds. And that's part of what I was after.

So that was what it was all about. A challenge to get really good at something in a set period of time against all the odds. A challenge to fulfil an old childhood dream. A challenge to change my life. And as I sit here now, with a brand new career as an author, and as an advisor to the restaurant and coffee-bar trade, and with a very different outlook on life, it's clear that it certainly did just that. And what's more, it has changed it for the better in almost every way.

And now I challenge you, not necessarily to look at your golf and address the comfort zone that you may have slipped into, but, much more importantly, to dig out an old dream and pursue it with everything you've got. Think back to that teenage version of yourself and the dreams and aspirations that you once had. There is bound to be something you once wanted to do, try out or achieve that you gradually put to one side because people repeatedly told you it wasn't possible, or a parent, sibling or friend dismissed as a silly notion. Perhaps you had an inadequate teacher at school who sucked a bit of life and enthusiasm out of you and put you off a subject that you might have otherwise enjoyed, or a boss who discouraged you from applying for a promotion or training opportunity you were keen on. Maybe from time to time you think about that dream or idea or subject or job and think to yourself: 'I wonder ...' or 'If only ...' or 'I wish ...' Well, you know, it's never too late. Take it from me. Resurrect that old passion or dream. Do it today.

Granted, very few of us have the relentless dedication of Michael Schumacher, Tiger Woods or Ben Hogan, or the raw talent of Seve Ballesteros or Ayrton Senna. Even fewer of us have the true grit of the amputee golfer Bob MacDermott. Most of us allow the daily grind of life and circumstances to trample on our dreams. But please don't let your final living thought on this earth be: 'I wish I had ...' Far better that it was, 'I'm so glad I did ...' And be sure to ignore anyone who says it isn't possible. Just go for it.

If golf is your thing and you want to improve your game radically, Seve is currently free from my duties, so by all means borrow him ...

Dream on.

Glossary

birdie – a score of one below par for a hole, e.g. completing a par three hole in two shots

bogey – a score of one shot over par for a hole, e.g. completing a par four hole in five shots

card a score – to submit a signed score card to a handicap committee or competition scorer. The card then counts towards your handicap.

cavity back iron – an iron with a largish head and a cavity or dent on the back of the face; a relatively 'easy to hit' style of iron

check spin – back spin on a wedge shot that makes the ball stop quickly

chip – a shot around the green that has a low trajectory of flight and that will run when it hits the ground

clubface – the part of the club that makes contact with the ball

drive – a shot taken with the driver; generally the longest shot a golfer can hit and the shot played when teeing off

driver head – the part of the driver that makes contact with the ball

eagle – a score of two below par for a hole, e.g. completing a par four hole in two shots

four-ball game – A group of four golfers all playing generally over 18 holes. The cornerstone of friendly golf matches.

gimme – a short putt that (in friendly matches) you don't have to play because it's considered so easy that you couldn't miss it. Counts as one shot. Not allowed in competition play.

grooving – the process of practising a new change in your swing so that it becomes permanent

handicap – the numerical measure of a golfer's playing ability. This complicated system means that golfers can play matches on an equal footing regardless of ability. A golfer with a handicap of thirteen plays a round in an average of thirteen shots over par. Sometimes expressed as 'S/he plays off thirteen.'

hook – a shot that veers badly to the left (for a right-handed golfer)

hybrid club – a club that is relatively easy to hit and which can be used for a variety of situations, e.g. to chip with or replace a long iron. A recent invention.

iron – the clubs that are used most from the fairway (or tee) to hit the ball onto the green. Traditionally – before the development of hybrid clubs and wedges – this label covered all clubs between a one iron and a pitching wedge.

lie – the piece of grass that the ball lands on. A good lie will be easy to hit from, a bad lie will be difficult.

lipped putt – a putt that just catches the edge of the hole but fails to go in

mulligan – when you're playing with friends, and miss or fluff a shot, your playing partners can give you a mulligan, i.e. let you take the shot again without penalty and without counting the duff shot in your score. Only applies in friendly games of golf (never in competition) and only once per round (usually only on a drive).

par; level par – an estimated standard score for a hole or course that a good player should be able to make. A par three hole should be completed in three shots. A level par round is when a player goes round in a prescribed number of shots, e.g. going round a par-seventy-two course in seventy-two shots.

pitch – a shot around the green with a high trajectory which will generally stop quickly when it hits the ground

plug – a ball which is buried in the grass on a wet course, or in the sand in a bunker

putt – a shot played with the putter on the green

rib – a shot hit with the leading edge of the clubface; not a good shot

rough – the areas of vegetation and longer unkempt grass on a golf course

scratch golfer – a player who shoots an average of par; the equivalent of a handicap of zero

shag bag – a bag filled with practice balls

shank – a shot where the ball connects with the hosel (the part of the club where the club head meets the shaft) rather than the clubface and shoots off violently to the right; a truly horrible shot

slice – a very common shot among high handicappers; the ball starts relatively straight but quickly veers off to the right

spraying – randomly hitting shots to the left or right with no consistent direction

Stableford points system – a scoring system, commonly used in amateur competition, that allows golfers to receive points for each hole. These points are added up to make the final score, rather than the number of shots. It negates the effects of a couple of really bad holes because the player isn't penalised by being more than one over par.

thin – a ball struck by the leading edge of the clubface (generally not quite as bad as a rib)

top the ball – a terrible shot; the bottom of the club comes in contact with the ball and not the clubface

wedge: sand, lob, gap – a variety of clubs that help to get the ball close to the hole from different circumstances in and around the green

Acknowledgements

My thank you list encompasses both the golf challenge, and the writing and publication of this book. As I look back over the project I am amazed at just how many people have helped and supported me along the way. It is quite humbling for me to recall all the conversations with these people, and the time and energy that many of them invested in my personal crusade. Of course this list is by no means exhaustive, and my apologies and thanks in equal measure go to those who aren't mentioned.

Firstly, I have to thank Lesley and Aimee for allowing me without complaint (almost) to indulge myself so fully for the challenge year.

Special thanks must also go to the trio of people without whom it simply wouldn't have been possible – Debbie Hanna, Stuart Kennedy and David Walters. I owe you all an enormous debt of gratitude.

Then, in no particular order, I sincerely thank ... Patrick, Katriona, Rosemary and Peter Richardson; Gordon Rea; Michael Donald; all the JustGoFaster boys but in particular Mark Tortolano, John Allan and Sean Fazackerly; Chris Johnson; Frank Farnschlaeder; Darren Greenan; Jeremy and Louise Hinds; Annick Lentacker; Dr Carey Mumford; Mark McMurray; Jim Mclellan; Richard Gibson; Nick Cann; Paul Fields; William McDowell; Herbie; John Short; Liam Kelly; Duncan Lennard; Michael Bannon; Rory McIlroy; Tony White; Bob MacDermott; Karl Morris; Darren Clarke; Seve Ballesteros; Ben Hogan; Sam Torrance; Nick Faldo; Padraig Harrington; Bob Cullen;

Bob Rotella; Bill Cullen; Andy Brown; Peanuts; Onabreak; Willow; Paul Smith; Mau; my agents Paul and Susan Feldstein; and my editor Helen Wright and all the team at Blackstaff.